The Taming Of The C.A.N.D.Y.☆ Monster

a cookbook by Vicki Lansky

☆Continuously, Advertised, Nutritionally, Deficient, Yummies!

How to Get Your Kids to Eat Less
Sugary, Salty Junk Foods ...

Without Sacrificing Convenience
Or Good Taste

Illustrations by Lynn Johnston

Meadowbrook Press

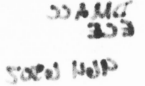

First Printing February 1978
Second Printing March 1978
Third Printing April 1978

Copyright©1978 by Vicki Lansky

Published by

Meadowbrook Press, 16648 Meadowbrook Lane, Wayzata, MN. 55391
ISBN 0-915658-08-9 (quality paperback)
Printed in the United States of America

ACKNOWLEDGEMENTS

A cookbook develops in the kitchen
as well as out of the kitchen.

My special thanks go to:

Claire Prosser . . . for recipe development and testing
Dr. Jack Anderson . . . a knowledgeable nutritionally-oriented,
  pediatric dentist
Dr. Mitch Einzig . . . a personable pediatric gastrointestinal
  specialist
Vernal Packard . . . a sharing food scientist from the
  University of Minnesota
Bev Kees . . . an erudite editor
Janet Sadlack . . . a microwave maven
Margaret Burgess . . . for her ABC's on our IBM
Bob Burgess . . . for his significant book title contribution
Ellen Gold . . . a friend and home economist who married a
  milk-intolerant doctor

Recipe thanks go to: Kathy Johnson
                      Meredith Berg
                      Friske Louw
                      Jill and Julie Segal
                      Kathleen Dalton
                      Jan Bakken
                      R. Henne
                      Elizabeth Holey
                      Aunt Betty (Booth)

TO

DOUG AND DANA

my tireless tasters who always insure
that our lives are kept in perspective

and to

BRUCE

my love, my business partner,
my best critic, my husband,
and most important . . .
my best friend.

CONTENTS

Page

NUTRITION IS A MATTER OF PARENTING 1

BROWN-BAGGING IT TO SCHOOL 15
Bringing Treats to School 25
Your School Lunch Program 29

TASTY ALTERNATIVES TO JUNK-FOOD SNACKS . . 31
Frozen 33
Dippy 36
Crunchy 37
Just Plain Good 42
Snack Drinks 46

IT'S DELICIOUS...It's (more) Nutritious...IT'S DESSERT . . 53
Frostings 68

SITTER SELECTIONS . . .Food, That Is 77

EATING ENROUTE 85
Drinks 86
Fast Food Restaurants 88

COOKING FOR KIDS IN A MICROWAVE 93

IF YOUR CHILD CAN'T DRINK MILK 103
Breakfast 107
Lunch 108
Desserts 110

TO MARKET—A Selective Guide For Parents 115
Produce 117
Cans And Jars 120
Cereals 121
Baby Food 128
Dairy 130
Beverages 132

CONTEMPORARY GLOSSARY OF KITCHEN TERMS . . 137
INDEX

Nutrition
Is A Matter
Of Parenting

C.A.N.D.Y. (Continuously Advertised Nutritionally Deficient Yummies), sweet desserts and fast food restaurants have a magical appeal to my children. With hundreds of millions of advertising dollars aimed directly at them, I am not surprised. I know what my kids would do with the grocery money if they did the shopping, and where they would like to eat if I didn't plan on cooking—and it's not at Grandma's!

Alarmist food scares appearing in the media almost daily make it very difficult for parents concerned about the quality and safety of the foods we buy to know whether we are making nutritious food selections. The list of potentially harmful foods continues to grow. EVERYTHING SEEMS TO BE MAKING THE FORBIDDEN LIST! Most of us don't really believe that all these overly sweetened, salted and fatty/fried foods we're warned against are really all that bad. After all, who ever heard of someone dying from an overdose of potato chips? And even the "experts" don't agree. How is it possible to deal intelligently with the flood of conflicting information on nutrition? The apparent choices are either to make a leap-of-faith into the health food camp or to continue with suicidal bravado down the aisle filling our grocery carts with the usual selection of "unsafe" (?) foods.

I find myself in the middle of this dilemma. My young son is the original C.A.N.D.Y. monster and his younger sister is a close copy. I have come to believe that many packaged convenience foods are not my best nutritional buy. Yet, as a busy, non-kitchen-oriented mother of two, I don't think I should have to trade good taste and convenience for better nutrition. How does one decide which foods to buy and which to avoid?

The more I read, the more I recognize how greatly publicity adds credibility to any "new" food information that comes along. Oftentimes the information is theory, not fact. But how and where does one find the *Truth* — if it is even known? Doctors provide us with few specifics unless we're on a special diet. Their advice is generally limited to the admonition, "Eat a balanced diet." But what does that really mean? They say it is a diet emphasizing protein foods, dairy foods, fresh fruits and vegetables, and whole grain foods; and that no one food contains all the nutrients we need, which is why variety is essential. True! But they usually fail to add that good health is not encouraged by unnecessary consumption of candy, cakes, cookies, chips, highly sweetened cereals, pop, powdered and canned soft drinks, etc.; and that kids (and parents) should lighten up on fried foods, pasta, white bread and rolls. They check children's tonsils but not their junk food consumption. When was the last time your pediatrician asked about your child's diet?

2

Nutrition is seldom studied in depth in medical school. One doctor told me that his major nutritional education in medical school covered scurvy and rickets—two diseases he has yet to see among his patients. Doctors are trained to treat illness, not to prevent it.

This puts the responsibility right back on us as parents. We are, after all, the shoppers and providers; and what is more important for parents to do than to nurture and nourish our children? Nutrition relates directly to growth, health, learning ability and general well-being.

Parents, as well as consumer advocates and nutritionists, seem bothered most by the substances ADDED to the foods we eat. Today, the word "additive" conjures up a negative image. Actually, an additive is *anything* added in manufacturing, preparing, treating or storing food. The same vitamin A you eat in a carrot becomes an additive when it is extracted and put in another product. Sugar dropped in your iced tea or coffee is an additive. The flavorings of sugarless gum are additives as are the colorings that go into cheeses. Additives receiving the most attention are those that make possible all the convenience foods we've come to depend upon. Additives are needed for flavor, texture, appearance and shelf-life. They facilitate food preparation, make many foods readily available and maintain food values by preventing spoilage. On the other hand, some are used to disguise inferior processing, conceal inferior ingredients and deceive us by making fabricated foods appear to be the real thing.

BUT ARE ADDITIVES DANGEROUS? I'm not the expert, but it appears that most additives are safe; some are questionable. For me the key to developing nutritional priorities lies in an examination of the **quantity** of additives we eat. Food scientists agree that anything in great quantity can be dangerous, sometimes cancer-causing, even lethal. Salt can be toxic and so can caffeine when consumed in excessive dosages. Many of the foods we ingest have a natural toxicity but are dangerous only in excess. While no additives we eat have been proven to cause cancer in humans, some studies using animals indicate possible danger.

3

Since I have taken quantity as a key criterion of safety, let us examine the quantity of additives we actually ingest:

Additive	1975 per capita annual consumption*
White Refined Sugar	90 pounds
corn syrup and dextrose	24 pounds
	114 pounds total sugars
salt	15 pounds
saccharin	7 pounds
everything else	10 pounds

*Source: "Food Consumption, Prices and Expenditures—'75 supplement." U.S. Department of Agriculture, "Processed Foods and the Consumer," V. Parkard, University of Minnesota Press, 1976.

By the way, the average per capita consumption of refined sugar in 1900 was between 20-60 lbs. Offical government records were not kept in 1900 for this item so estimates vary. But the greatest controversies surround those additives far down on the consumption list. Until recently the most commonly consumed additives have been relatively ignored.

"Everything else" includes yeast, pepper, mustard, sodium bicarbonate, citric acid, MSG and 27 other such additives which account for nine of the 10 pounds. The last pound of the 10 includes colorings, emulsifiers, preservatives, etc., from a possible 1,800 different chemical compounds.

SUGAR

The sugar listed above is the white refined stuff made from cane or beet. Sugar found naturally in foods is not an additive and is not included in the list above. Your family of four will consume over 450 pounds of sugar additives this year, if your diet is typical. How can this be? Think of the number of bags of groceries you carry into your home. Nearly every box, bottle, can and bagged item that you buy contains added refined sugar. Most sodas, sauces, crackers, cakes, sherbets and ice creams—as well as cereals, breads, dressings and drinks—have sugar added.

DO YOU KNOW HOW MUCH SUGAR IS HIDDEN IN THESE COMMON FOODS?

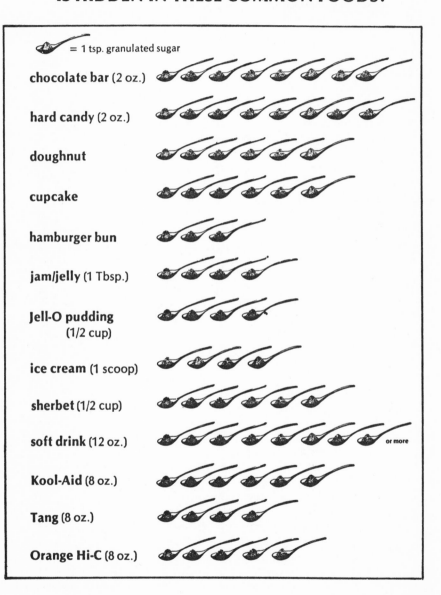

= 1 tsp. granulated sugar

chocolate bar (2 oz.)

hard candy (2 oz.)

doughnut

cupcake

hamburger bun

jam/jelly (1 Tbsp.)

Jell-O pudding
(1/2 cup)

ice cream (1 scoop)

sherbet (1/2 cup)

soft drink (12 oz.) or more

Kool-Aid (8 oz.)

Tang (8 oz.)

Orange Hi-C (8 oz.)

In fact, 70 percent of the sugar we eat is hidden in the products we buy. If sugars were just a small part of our diet, it wouldn't be of such concern, but 114 pounds intake per person is A LOT! There is no physiological requirement for refined sugar that cannot be satisfied by other more nutritious foods. And no authority will claim that a sugar-free diet is dangerous.

Sugar is 100 percent pure as advertised. Pure calories, that is— and nothing else. Sugar offers NO vitamins, minerals or trace elements. This refined carbohydrate is used by your body as energy or stored as fat. It does not contribute to growing strong and healthy bodies.

Most doctors acknowledge sugar's most obvious negative— causing dental cavities. Medical research is now linking our society's high sugar intake to diabetes, obesity, hypoglycemia, heart disease and even mental health problems. For more detailed studies of the potential dangers of sugar I suggest reading:

SWEET AND DANGEROUS by J. Yudkin (Bantam 1973)

SUGAR BLUES by W. Dufty (Warner 1976)

While I accept all the negatives intellectually, I am not able— at least yet—to completely eliminate refined sugar from my diet or that of my children. I find that there are many parents who share my dilemma. We are at one place in our heads and another in reality. So I deal with this fact by saying that, while none is probably best, LESS is at least BETTER.

Here are some "handles" I have found helpful in reducing my family's sugar intake:

1) Use sugar substitutes whenever possible. I have kept granulated artificial sweetner in our sugar bowl, but the possible banning of saccharin may change this.

2) Decrease the amount of sugar called for in a recipe. You can usually decrease a recipe by up to a 1/4 cup of sugar called for without affecting texture in recipes in other books. Sometimes adding extra vanilla flavoring will compensate for lessening the sugar called for.

3) Look for recipes that call for less sweetening (all types), not more, (such as you will find in this book and "FEED ME! I'M YOURS").

(continued on next page)

4)   Don't treat dessert as the final act of every meal. I know one family that serves dessert only twice a week—on weekends.
5)   Read labels while grocery shopping, or even after you get your purchases home. This has helped change my shopping habits.
6)   Screen children's food requests in the grocery store. A treat can be a piece of fruit or a pack of sugarless gum.
7)   Don't be afraid to say NO! to your children. (I'm not too consistent about this.)
8)   Don't just say "NO"! Explain the whys and wherefores. Try to remember to add, "No! because I love you and I want you to grow up to be strong and healthy."
9)   Discuss TV ads aimed at children with your children. Explain the company's motivation and possible half-truths mentioned.
10) Try to decrease your reliance on packaged foods. A bit of extra thought and planning is involved.
11) Keep convenient portable snack foods on hand. A fruit plate on the table, nuts in a jar, cut-up vegetables in the refrigerator cooler and cut-up pieces of cheese in a plastic bag in the refrigerator.
12) MOST IMPORTANT!!! DON'T KEEP C.A.N.D.Y. IN THE HOUSE. That's the only way to insure that junk food is not a major part of your children's daily calorie intake.

I meet more and more parents who are not allowing their children to be exposed to refined sugar products. These people feel very strongly that their children don't crave and/or demand C.A.N.D.Y. As the children grow older, these foods often seem too sweet and are not missed. I myself did not feel as strongly about what my children ate when they were younger as I do now, so I have been working to change our food choices. My children don't care for what I broadly refer to as "health foods." They reject the taste and texture of many of these foods. And I reject the extra cost. Yet they love whole wheat bread, nuts, fresh fruits and hard cheeses.

Honey has been touted by health food enthusiasts as the healthy answer to the sweet tooth. Interestingly, honey has more calories and is sweeter than refined sugar. Many honey enthusiasts are convinced that honey is a superior food nutritionally. The nutritional value of honey may be sizeable for bees but the amount available for human use is small. On balance, however, I do believe that honey is preferable to sugar because:

1) It is said to metabolize more slowly—rather than with refined sugar's lightning speed—so that it plays less havoc with one's insulin and blood sugar level.
2) Its cost and (for many) its taste are self-limiting.
3) Because it is sweeter than sugar—less is needed.
4) With the possibility that saccharin may be banned because it may cause cancer in test animals, our choice of sweeteners becomes narrower.

Brown sugar is a mite better than white refined sugar but only a "baby step" so. The brown comes from a trace of molasses added. Originally brown sugar was sugar with the molasses not completely processed out, but today it is made by returning some of the molasses to regular refined sugar. Still, the molasses does give it a bit of extra food value. Brown sugar even has slightly fewer calories than white sugar.

Since all sweeteners have much in common against them, the obvious course to adopt is MODERATION. We all tend to think we live moderately. The best way I can suggest to test your sugar consumption is to serve your family—for just one day—NOTHING MADE WITH REFINED SUGAR. I think you will find it very frustrating. You will have to read every label because you can take nothing for granted in our pre-sweetened world.

SALT

Salt is the second most prevalent additive in our diet. Salt seems to be in everything, as the person on a salt-free diet soon finds out. And the salt added to most packaged foods is usually not the iodized salt that prevents goiter caused by an iodine deficiency of the thyroid gland.

Salt is important in the regulation of our internal fluid balance. Originally used to preserve foods, salt is used now mainly as a flavor enhancer. In fact, it really is a cultural taste habit which has grown to such proportions that it seems to have become an actual threat to our health.

8

Salt (which is all forms of sodium) when taken in excess— which seems to be what we in America are doing—is suspected of being the primary cause of hypertension in adults. Hypertension, strongly related to heart disease, affects more than 20 million people in this country. At an annual per capita consumption rate of 15 pounds, we are each consuming at least the equivalent of one round 26 ounce container of salt monthly, or 10-15 grams a day. Nutritionists agree that we should have no more than 3 grams of sodium a day, which is a bit more than a 1/4 tsp. Studies have shown that people who use very little salt are practically free from high blood pressure. Now, since you probably purchase only one to three boxes of table salt a year, you can imagine how much salt must come from packaged and restaurant foods.

In many ways I find it harder to deal successfully with salt than with sugar. Despite the fact that table salt is not used in our home and that salt is used infrequently in cooking (it is required in baking because its chemical interaction with yeast controls the rising), I'm still sure that we consume too much of it. We avoid obvious items such as potato chips and French fries but I know we eat salt every time we eat cheese, nuts (most commercial varieties are salted), canned vegetables or diet soda. Obviously, the more you avoid packaged convenience foods, the more salt you will avoid. Most recipes that call for salt do so out of tradition. Now is a good time to start changing this cooking habit. Even if salt were never added to foods we would probably get all we need because salt (not iodized salt) occurs naturally in many foods such as milk, meat and eggs, to name a few.

Keep in mind that while fresh meats and poultry are relatively low in sodium, this is not the case with ham, bacon, sausage and hot dogs. Fresh fish is low in sodium but canned fishes, such as tuna, are high.

If you are not ready to do without table salt completely, try "LITE-SALT" which has a lower sodium content and does contain iodine. Also when buying garlic seasonings, pick garlic powder over garlic salt.

FOODS WITH A NATURAL LOW SODIUM CONTENT

Item	Sodium (g/100g)
oranges	.002
cranberries	.004
watermelon	.008
apples	.010
asparagus	.017
pears	.019
green peas	.022
grapes	.022
blueberries	.025
onions	.025
rice	.014
corn	.016
potatoes	.010-25

FOODS WITH A NATURAL HIGH SODIUM CONTENT

Item	Sodium (g/100g)
raisins	.120
olives	.090
Swiss cheese	.850
egg	.058
cow's milk	.045
cottage cheese	.030
white bread	.280
brown rice	.160
condensed milk	.200
cucumbers	.125
tomatoes	.125
carrots	.120

Source: SALT-FREE NUTRITION PLAN Bircher-Benner, Nash Publishing, 1967.

EVERYTHING ELSE

Labels tell an astonishing story. Our foods seem to be "filled" with additives. Anything other than the base ingredient—and usually that, too—must be listed on the label. These additives may be natural or chemical in origin. Natural additives include salt, sugar, wheat germ, etc. Chemical additives can be a combination of real foods or laboratory duplications. But chemicals are the stuff everything is made of. All the nutrients of our diet—the proteins, carbohydrates, fats and vitamins—are chemical compounds. Ascorbic acid is vitamin C and vitamin C is ascorbic acid. Natural vanilla flavoring, however, does not have the same chemical base as artificial vanilla flavoring. All additives, natural or fabricated, are regulated by the Food and Drug Administration (FDA) and are restricted as to their use and quantity in various foods. Despite the fact that most additives are safe, it has been alarming for the consumer to note that the FDA has changed its mind on occasion and banned certain additives, such as Red Dye #2, previously considered safe.

Dr. Benjamin Feingold states in his book, WHY YOUR CHILD IS HYPERACTIVE (Bookworks, 1975) that artificial colorings and flavorings cause an "allergic" reaction in children which is known as hyperactivity. Since most parents feel that their children are hyperactive—at least those of us who prefer a quieter existence —what better motivation do you need? While Dr. Feingold's studies have not been duplicated successfully to the satisfaction of the medical community, many parents across the country have duplicated his diet recommendations with apparent success. I do not know how valid his thesis will ultimately prove to be, but if you are interested in information about the diet and finding a support group of parents in your area, write to The Feingold Association, 56 Winston Drive, Smithtown, New York, 11787. Send a stamped self-addressed legal size envelope. It is a volunteer organization so allow 4-6 weeks for a reply.

☆   ☆   ☆

I know I have treated all these concerns about food additives very superficially. In many ways this is unbalanced and unfair. There are many issues I have not even mentioned. However, this introduction is not intended to be a complete nutritional dissertation but rather an explanation of my reasons for selecting the recipes and topics that follow.

I don't perceive myself as a cook (the less time in the kitchen, the better) or a food expert. Mainly I am a mother searching for better and more acceptable ways to feed my family. I have come to accept the fact that the only way to avoid many additives (primarily sugar) is to stay away from highly processed foods whenever possible. I have learned that it is not inconvenient to serve a box of raisins or a hunk of cheese for a snack, or to serve a quality ice cream for dessert. It becomes a question of trying to implement my priorities. I try to maximize food value and convenience without minimizing taste. I feel it is possible to serve appealing alternatives using widely available foods.

Food that goes uneaten cannot nourish. In selecting the recipes for this book, an important criterion has been kid acceptability. While I have tried to use recipes that are consistently lower in refined sugar, it has not always been possible. Some recipes contain more sweeteners than I like to serve but these at least have some nutritional advantages over C.A.N.D.Y.—the foods they are meant to replace. Salt is only used in recipes where it is vital. My selections are intended to give you a range of alternatives from which to choose, not to earn a certificate of nutritional purity (whatever that is). One must weigh cost, preparation time and nutritional value against what will actually be consumed.

You may or may not be where I'm at. You may be getting there or you may have passed me long ago. But for those of you who are struggling to make intelligent market (grocery, that is) decisions, I hope my information and recipes will help you along. Selecting good foods for one's family is not an easy task. We carry our own food prejudices based on what our mothers fed us, what our spouses want on the table, what our children will condescend to eat, and what our pockets can afford.

We are a new generation of mothers whose "nutrition-consciousness" has been raised. We are not "health food faddists" but concerned parents who still wish to experience good-tasting food without sacrificing the health of our families.

SOME OF THE CHAPTERS IN THIS BOOK MAY NOT SEEM APPLICABLE TO YOU. I DO HOPE YOU WILL GLANCE THROUGH THESE CHAPTERS ANY—WAY AS I THINK YOU WILL FIND MANY OF THE RECIPES WORTHWHILE. THANK YOU (V.L.)

Brown Bagging It

A short while ago you were leaving your child with a bottle and a sitter. Now s/he is leaving you with lunch in hand for nursery school, kindergarten or grade school. More often than not, Mom's lunch will be preferred, if not actually demanded. You will probably hit upon a few favorites plus a variety of fruits and vegetables that will make your child's APPROVED LIST. Do not be surprised when you discover that much trading and switching goes on over lunch tables. It's the American Way. But too often we hear that sandwiches end up in the wastebasket, desserts are eaten first, and "side dishes" are left on the side. If you are getting this kind of feedback, the time has come for a re-evaluation of what you are packing into the lunch bag.

Your child's choice of a lunch pack container will be determined by the peer group. Sometimes the fashionable lunch box is "in," and other times the brown paper bag is. There are pros and cons for each. The box, while more expensive, keeps sandwiches from getting squished and holds a thermos. The bag is cheaper but may be considered unecological. On special outings, a bag is a better selection than the forgettable-in-the-excitement lunch box.

Variety may not be important to every school-age child. One child will insist on peanut butter sandwiches for lunch every day while another prefers a variety. As for Mom, there are advantages to each approach and nothing absolute about either.

The lunch you pack should include:

A PROTEIN RICH FOOD

A FRUIT OR VEGETABLE

SOMETHING EXTRA (I hate to classify it as dessert)

A BEVERAGE

FOOD FOR THOUGHT (optional)

A PROTEIN RICH FOOD

Lunch bags are not legally required to contain sandwiches, Besides, the bread, when it is made primarily of white flour, may be more of a filler than a nutritious food.

Consider packing in small plastic bags:

Cheese—a hunk or slices

Nuts—a variety including peanuts, cashews, almonds, etc., alone or with raisins, sunflower seeds, pumpkin seeds, etc.

Peanut butter—stuffed into an apple or celery sticks

Cottage cheese or cheese spread—in celery sticks or cucumber boats

Tuna salad or egg salad—in celery sticks or cucumber boats, or wrapped in a lettuce leaf

Chicken or turkey—cubes, wings or drumsticks

Meat—in pieces, slices or cubes

Meatloaf slice

Hard-cooked eggs—shelled for the younger child

Yogurt

16

Most kids are quite happy to discover proteins such as luncheon meats, sliced ham and beef jerky in their lunch bags. However the label reading parent quickly discovers that along with the protein these foods also contain nitrates, salt, preservatives, and sometimes corn syrup and other sugars. If you use them, think of them as a "change of pace" to be used in moderation.

Remember to keep the normally refrigerated foods in the refrigerator until your child is leaving for school.

PEANUT BUTTER BALLS
    1/2 cup (7 Tbsp.) peanut butter
    1/2 cup honey (consider using part molasses here)
    1 cup toasted wheat germ
    2 Tbsp. powdered milk
Mix ingredients well, into balls, then roll in coconut (optional) or pat flat in a pan as for fudge. Refrigerate.

Variation: Press between two squares of Chex cereal.

Or in a wide mouth thermal jug:
    A hefty soup
    Frankfurter in hot soup
    Macaroni and cheese
    Chili
You may wish to include a moist towelette as well as a napkin. Or maybe both are wishful thinking!

SANDWICHES

Sandwiches are the versatile, flexible and traditional vehicle for providing protein rich foods. A sandwich is usually 60 percent bread, so it is important that you use a good bread. A good bread is made of enriched flour rather than plain white flour. A better bread is made of whole wheat or other whole grain flour.

Why is whole wheat flour in our bread important? Wheat, the basic ingredient in bread products, consists of a core encrusted in an outer brown covering called bran, and a small section known as the wheat germ. Towards the end of the 19th century, millers found that by changing from stone wheels to steel rollers, it was possible to inexpensively separate the outer covering of the wheat containing the bran and wheat germ from the kernel, leaving white flour. It made very light baked goods and had a very long shelf life. Most of the wheat's important value, however, is contained in the bran and the wheat germ. The bran covering provides fiber and bulk plus essential minerals and some vitamins. Wheat germ, besides being a good source of vitamin E and the vitamin B family, is high in protein, calcium, iron and phosphorous. Millers were not overly concerned that much of the nutritional benefits had been processed out because white flour was a commercial success.

In 1941 the United States government set standards for the enrichment of white flour but they called for putting back only a few of the 22 nutrients that had been milled out. Those restored were put back in at their level of strength present before refinement. They were thiamin, riboflavin, niacin and iron, but none of the other essential minerals and vitamins were replaced. So today we have enriched flour. While it certainly is better to buy enriched flour than flour not enriched, whole wheat flour is far more nutritious because all the "enrichment" is there naturally.

So, if you want the school sandwich to offer more per bite, whole wheat bread is the place to start. Your children don't like whole grain breads? Don't make the transition overnight. Start with a light whole grain bread which contains both whole wheat and enriched white flour. Experiment. Read labels carefully. Don't equate a dark bread with whole wheat. Often caramel coloring is used to give the appearance of whole wheat bread. No need to announce the new plan. Work at it gradually unless going "cold turkey" is more effective for you. Kids will eat what is there, especially when they realize after a few days that they have no alternative.

In the following list of ideas, remember that the major protein value will come from what you put between the slices of bread and not from the bread itself.

18

PEANUT BUTTER SANDWICHES
Peanut butter* with:
  honey
  sliced bananas
  grated carrots and raisins
  applesauce
  bacon bits and honey
  cream cheese and jam/jelly
  toasted wheat germ and honey
  cut-up dates
  carob frosting (see page 70)
  or any combination of the above

   Peanut butter sandwiches freeze well and are easy to make ahead. They are especially easy to make on bread still frozen. Make a batch on Sunday night, or just make extras while you're preparing lunches some unhurried morning (Good luck!). In fact, buy an extra loaf for just this purpose. Make up the whole loaf (do not slice sandwiches) and return them to the original plastic bag and store in the freezer. Remove as needed—slice—and wrap to go.

   Peanut butter can also be spread on graham crackers as a sandwich.

   IMPORTANT: Yes, there are actually children who DO NOT LIKE peanut butter. No need to rush to your nearest psychiatrist! There are documented cases of normal development among such children.

*See page 120 for tips from the "To Market" chapter on what to look for when buying peanut butter.

TUNA FISH SANDWICHES
Tuna fish, mayonnaise and:
  pickle relish
  sliced cucumbers
  sunflower seeds
  sprouts
  sliced egg
  sliced avacado
  grated carrot
  chopped celery

(continued on next page)

19

Mayonnaise in a sandwich does not hold up well. It turns rancid upon prolonged exposure to heat. Avoid using it for summer camp lunches, or if your child's lunch will be sitting on a radiator in school all morning. Mayonnaise usually does not freeze well. If the amount you are using in your sandwich mix is small, however, you should have no trouble keeping sandwiches mixed with mayonnaise in the freezer. This also holds true for egg salad that is well mashed.

Making your own mayonnaise really isn't hard if you have a blender. Commercial mayonnaise doesn't have a list of ingredients on the label so you really know what you are getting when you make your own.

BLENDER MAYONNAISE
    1 egg or 2 egg yolks
    2 Tbsp. lemon juice or white vinegar
    1/4 tsp. salt
    1/2 tsp. dry mustard
    1 cup vegetable oil

Combine all ingredients in the blender except the oil. Blend to the count of 7. Add 1/4 cup of oil, cover and blend to the count of 7 again. If the oil is combined, you should hear a slurping sound as you remove the cover. Scrape down the sides with a rubber spatula and repeat this procedure using a 1/4 cup oil at a time until all the oil is combined with the mixture. Store in a covered glass container in the refrigerator. In fact an old, clean mayonnaise jar is perfect.

If you plan to add lettuce (and your child plans to eat it) it is better wrapped separately in the lunch bag for placing in the sandwich just before it's to be eaten.

CREAM CHEESE SANDWICHES
Cream cheese and:
    brown (canned) sliced nutbread
    raisins—whole or ground
    bacon bits and crushed pineapple
    chopped nuts
    luncheon meats
    peanut butter
    sliced egg
    sliced cucumber
    marmalade or jam

Unlike most other cheese, cream cheese does not have a high protein value though it does have a high fat content. Combining cream cheese with other protein foods would provide a more nutritious sandwich. Also, cream cheese spreads with greater success on sliced frozen bread. For a change, serve it on raisin bread!

One enrichment technique is to mix a tablespoon of powdered milk into an 8-ounce bar of cream cheese.

DO-IT-YOURSELF GRAPE JELLY

Somewhere back in history, jelly became a must in both peanut butter and cream cheese sandwiches. If you have ever made jelly yourself you know that sugar is the major ingredient. In fact, so much sugar goes into making jellies and jams that you always need to buy extra. But here is a recipe for making your own grape jelly that, while not sugarless, contains far less sugar than is used in those commercial products. With this recipe you also eliminate the use of artificial colorings and flavorings.

Method #1

    1 (12-oz.) can frozen grape juice concentrate
    1/2 (1 3/4 oz.) pkg. of Slim Set*

Add one half of the Slim Set box to the thawed frozen grape juice concentrate. Heat to boiling. Simmer together for one minute, then remove from heat to cool. Pour into a wide mouth jar and refrigerate.

*Slim Set is a jelling mix that jells liquids without the aid of sugar. It is usually found in the grocery section with canning supplies. (Available from A-W Brands Inc., Carteret, N.J. 07008 and MCP Foods, Anaheim, Calif. 92805.)

Method #2

    1 (12-oz.) can frozen grape juice concentrate
    1 envelope unflavored gelatin

Dissolve the gelatin in the defrosted juice concentrate. Pour the mixture into a saucepan and heat to boiling or until the gelatin dissolves. Remove from heat, cool slightly, then pour into a wide mouth jar. Refrigerate.

This jelly does not spread as easily as the first method, but it still works well.

To make a completely sugarless jelly, use frozen apple juice concentrate or Tree Top's frozen grape/pear juice concentrate.

SANDWICH SPREADS

Here's hoping you have some tried-and-true spread recipes that your children like. I have only two! The major advantage of the first one is that it requires opening only one jar when preparing a sandwich—a small but significant point.

PEANUT-BUTTER-LIKE-NO-OTHER
Combine:

> 1 cup (14 Tbsp.) peanut butter
> 1/4 cup powdered milk
> 2 1/2 Tbsp. honey
> 1/2 cup toasted wheat germ
> 1/2 mashed banana

HOME-MADE CHEESE WHIZ (great for sandwiches, snacks and traveling, too!)

> 2 Tbsp. butter or margarine
> 1 1/2 lbs. American processed cheese
> 2 egg yolks, beaten
> 1 (13 oz.) can of evaporated milk
> 1 Tbsp. flour

In a double boiler, melt butter and add cheese. When softened, add egg yolks, milk and flour. Cook till thick. Store in a covered jar in the refrigerator.

HINT: Use this melted over cooked macaroni

A deli-meat sandwich is a good occasional sandwich if your budget allows.

A FRUIT OR VEGETABLE

The obvious:

> pickles
> green pepper strips
> celery
> cucumber slices
> cherry tomatoes
> orange (quartered)
> apple (cored, halved and placed back together to minimize browning)

carrot sticks*
banana
fresh fruit in season
dried fruit
seedless grapes
peaches

Cut fruits, such as apples and peaches can be prevented from turning brown by putting lemon, orange, or grapefruit juice on the cut section.

*MAKE AHEAD IDEA: Slice several carrots into sticks & wrap in a dampened paper towel and store in a plastic bag.

The not-so-obvious:
mandarin orange sections*
green or black olives
small salad in container
applesauce in container
canned fruits* in glass baby food jar
vegetables with a dip in the bottom of the container
cubed watermelon*
Chinese pea pods (which, when packed frozen, will defrost by lunch time)
pineapple chunks in a container

*Include a toothpick.

SOMETHING SPECIAL

That something special—the treat that most kids look for first in their lunch pack—can be both good tasting and good for them.

Try:
raisins (bagged or boxed)
popcorn in a bag
pretzels (see recipe, page 45)
container of yogurt
granola bars (see recipe, page 39)

(continued on next page)

cheese and crackers in a package
Finger Jello (recipe, page 42)
sunflower seeds
"redeeming value" cookies such as:
    Nutter-Butters
    Fig Newtons
    Graham crackers
    Oatmeal cookies, etc., etc., etc.

If you're including some good homemade cookies, make them extra large when you bake. You'll find that one large cookie instead of two small ones has far more kid-appeal. See page 63.

Slice up any of your favorite dessert breads or cakes into individual portions, wrap well and freeze. Toss one into a lunch bag as needed. This is a good way to keep from eating up the leftovers yourself.

Hunt's makes "Snack Packs" that include sliced peaches and fruit cocktail. Although they are overly sugared, they are definitely preferable to the puddings.

If your children understand that it's because you love them that you are not including Twinkies, they will feel special in a positive way among their sugar-consuming peers. Really! (And, boy, does my son ever crave Twinkies!)

BEVERAGES

Milk
Apple juice (hot or cold)
Orange juice
Hot tea (weak) with orange juice

Most schools provide milk or drink for a nominal fee. Because of a government subsidy, your child can buy milk in school cheaper than you can provide it. If your child is "pocket-less" or forgetful, tape the milk money to the inside of the lunch box with masking tape.

A small can of fruit juice makes a good pack-along drink, although it is expensive on a per serving basis. Freeze the can before sending it off in the lunch bag. It will defrost in time for lunch.

Good drinks to include in a thermos are orange or apple juice. Hot soup is especially nice on a cold, wintery day. A cooked hot dog carried in soup can be transferred at lunchtime to a bun, also provided in the lunch pack, and be truly a hot hot dog.

FOOD FOR THOUGHT

On special occasions—or whenever you feel like doing something special, include a note ("You're terrific" or "I love you," or "Happy Birthday," etc.) a funny drawing, or a little toy or game. Egos need nourishment too!

Keep in mind that a six-year-old and up *can* assemble his/her lunch bag with wrapped ahead "makings."

BRINGING TREATS TO SCHOOL

Before long, even though you are not a homeroom mother, you will need to supply a treat for the WHOLE class for a birthday, a festive occasion, or just because it's your turn. So what will be both appropriate and nutritious?

Snacks really fall into different categories. Banana slices dipped in honey and rolled in toasted wheat germ, just don't make it as a child's birthday treat. Let's start with the good-and-fun school snack ideas that will serve 25-30 and leave the party ideas till the end.

FRUIT TREATS:
>orange slices (circular slices are more fun)
>apple slices spread with peanut butter
>fruit kabobs—canned and/or fresh served on toothpicks*
>bananas for children to slice and serve
>dried apricots (2 bags)
>>*or fruit alternated with cheese cubes.

CRUNCHY TREATS:

granola (store bought* or homemade) served in a small
plastic bag or cup

popcorn (store bought or homemade) served in a small
plastic bag or cup

"Crunchola" mixture (page 38) served in a small plastic
bag or cup

*You will need 2 (16 oz.) boxes for 25-30 children.

OTHER TREAT IDEAS:

Yummie Balls (page 42)

Finger Jello (page 42) double this recipe

pizza slices

large soft pretzels (see recipe page 45)

carrot sticks served with a dip (if setting is appropriate)

celery filled with peanut butter or cream cheese with
raisins ("ants")

quartered peanut butter open face sandwiches

And . . .

EGG SAILBOATS

1 doz. eggs, hard-cooked
1/2 cup mayonnaise
1 tsp. mustard
2 doz. toothpicks
one sheet of paper

Shell eggs, slice in half and remove yolks. Combine yolks
with mayonnaise and mustard and return a spoonful of mixture
to hollow of each egg white. Tape small paper triangles to toothpicks (or let your child do that part) and stick them in egg halves
prior to serving.

SCHOOL TIME DRINKS

Providing a good tasting, good-for-you affordable drink for a
classroom is not easy. The obviously convenient and economical
drinks (Hi-C, Tang, Kool-Aid, et al.) are usually rejected by those
wishing to provide a better food value drink. Access to refrigeration can also influence drink choices. The choice selection is
really not very wide, if you wish to avoid added sugars and have
a limited budget. Here it is:

milk

frozen orange juice concentrates, reconstituted

frozen grapefruit juice concentrates, reconstituted

unsweetened apple juice—gallon container or frozen
concentrate variety

icey water

PARTY FAVORS

If you're not planning on bringing a food treat to mark the occasion of that highest of high days—your child's birthday—a birthday favor can mark the occasion.

For each child, one or a combination of the following:

a balloon (always a hit!)

a piece of sugarless gum, individually wrapped

a pack of sugarless gum, if your budget allows

a new pencil or eraser

a new comb (from an inexpensive combination package)

a 6" ruler

But if food it must be, try:

PARTY POPCORN

While the number of marshmallows in this recipe does tend to boggle the mind, I rationalize their use by the inclusion of nuts and sunflower seeds.

10 cups popped popcorn

1/4 cup (1/2 stick) margarine or butter

1 (10 oz.) bag of marshmallows

1/2 cup sunflower seeds

1 cup nuts

Optional: 1/2 cup (7 Tbsp.) peanut butter

Melt the shortening in a 3-quart saucepan. Add marshmallows and cook over low heat till syrupy. Remove from heat. Add peanut butter, if using. Add popcorn, seeds and nuts, and stir till they are well coated.

• With buttered hands, form into balls and place in cupcake papers.

• Fill 20 to 25 (5 oz.) paper cups 1/2 full and add a popsicle stick for a handle. After cooled and hardened, run knife around inside of cup to loosen.

• Spread in a large shallow greased pan and press down with a spatula or wax paper. When cool, cut into bars. If you want larger bars you will need to make two batches.

For a festive variation, these balls, pops or bars can be perked up further with raisins, sprinkles or candles. Food colorings can be added to the "syrup" before adding the popcorn.

CANDY COOKIES (this recipe makes a large-size heavily sugared but very popular cookie)

    1 cup liquid corn oil
    1 cup brown sugar
    1/2 cup white sugar
    2 eggs, beaten
    2 tsp. vanilla
    2 1/4 cups flour (white, or half white and half whole wheat)*
    1 1/2 tsp. baking soda
    1 cup (or less) M & M candies

      *Use Triple Rich Formula (page 123)

Combine oil, sugars, eggs and vanilla. Mix dry ingredients together and combine with creamed mixture. Drop by the teaspoonful onto an ungreased cookie sheet. Flatten to not more than 2 inches in diameter. Decorate with 3-5 candies per cookie, half pressing them into the dough. It is imperative that the number of candies be the same for each cookie. Bake at 375 degrees for 8-10 minutes. It is common for the candies to crack. This recipe makes 2-4 dozen cookies depending on the size of your teaspoon.

AGGRESSION COOKIES

This time-honored classic oatmeal cookie can be enriched by using whole wheat flour in combination with white and it still tastes terrific.
Combine:

    3 cups brown sugar
    3 cups (6 sticks) butter or margarine
        (or any combination of the two)
    6 cups oatmeal, uncooked
    3 cups flour (white, whole wheat or half and half)
    1 Tbsp. baking soda

There is only one way to mix this and that is to use your hands and any other hands you can enlist. Knead until there aren't any lumps of butter. Roll the dough into small balls and place them on an ungreased cookie sheet. Flatten gently with a small fork. Bake 10-12 minutes at 350 degrees. Cool before removing from cookie sheet. This recipe makes between 10 and 15 dozen cookies, enough to serve two homeroom classes and still leave some for home snacks. If you have room, store some in your freezer.

If you're up to making a cake, try the chocolate cake recipe on page 65. It will make a large, low pan cake or two dozen cupcakes which you can then frost.

If you are bringing homemade cookies, top off a nutritious cookie with a smile face made by squeezing homemade frosting from the corner of a small plastic bag — corner snipped off, of course.

Some schools do not allow homemade treats to be served in the classroom. About the only alternative you have is to select such items as peanut butter cookies, oatmeal cookies, gingerbread, etc., from your local bakery.

YOUR SCHOOL'S LUNCH PROGRAM

The school lunch program, which you may or may not be using, is under scrutiny. An annual $400 million of wasted, uneaten food has alarmed both Congress and the Department of Agriculture, which administers the national school lunch program. All children are served standard portions despite different appetites and food preferences. Short lunch periods make for rushed meals and are hard for slow eaters.

Consumer groups are concerned about the high proportion of fats and starches in the meals, the highly processed tasteless foods, and the ready availability of cake, ice cream and chocolate milk.

Have lunch with your child at school one day to check the quality and the atmosphere. If you are interested in improving your school's lunch program, contact The Center for Science in the Public Interest (CSPI) at 1755 S Street N.W., Washington, D.C. 20009. For their "School Food Action Packet" send $1.50. Ask also for their catalog as they offer posters, books, a newsletter and much good information on "newtrition."

Tasty Alternatives to Junk Food Snacks

Many children, mine included, seem to snack all day long. This is not necessarily a bad thing. Many parents act as though one of the Ten Commandments reads, "Thou shalt eat three meals a day," but little children don't follow rules all that well. If their snacks are nutritious and they are not snacking too close to mealtime, snacking should not be a problem. Perhaps if you view snacks as mini-meals (but not crying or knee-injury solace) they will be easier to accept.

Regrettably, snacks are often things that come out of boxes and bags in the forms of candy and chips. They supply energy but not essential nutrients. They are fatty and filling food substitutes with little redeeming value. The challenge lies in trying to switch children from snacks with lesser food value to more wholesome ones.

Our society holds a strange belief, thanks to advertising by the sugar industry, that sugared treats are a better pick-me-up than protein-packed snacks. Untrue! Not only are protein snacks — pieces of cheese, for example — a more beneficial pick-me-up, but they continue their good work by staying with you longer and contributing to growing strong, healthy bodies. Snacks made primarily of sugar, artificial colorings and flavorings cannot make this claim.

31

It's almost un-American to deny children snacks of candy or chips, especially when they are snacking at someone else's house. In your own home, though, you can go a long way toward correcting the "candy is dandy" image. The best technique is NOT TO HAVE IT IN THE HOUSE. If you believe that your kids are really eating too many unnecessary foods, don't buy them!

More and more parents who restrict their small children's exposure to sugared treats tell me that their children don't seem to crave or request them. They report that their children's tastes adapt until they find candy too sweet and can't finish it. Adults I've met whose parents were nutrition-conscious often carry their parents' concern into adulthood.

It is hard for a child — anyone, for that matter — to understand that what tastes good is not necessarily good for you. One theory on why sweets are so appealing is based on the fact that human beings cannot make their own vitamin C but must consume it. Vitamin C occurs naturally in citrus fruits, some vegetables (green peppers, for one), berries and leaves—foods which also have a sweet taste. Through evolution our taste buds may have been guided to foods which were sweet because they were good for us. But white refined sugar (not a naturally occurring foodstuff) contains no vitamin C, yet we consume it as though our lives depended on it.

What do you do about the child who walks into your house carrying candy, or when your child goes next door and is offered a sugary treat? You can realistically concern yourself only with what is brought into your house and not worry about what is eaten at a neighbor's. When sweets are brought into our house, I allow one taste, then remove them to a secure place until it is time for the guest to take them home. If you are confident that sweets are not a basic part of your child's diet, you can probably do more harm than good by making them forbidden food outside the home.

I resent most TV commercials that equate sugar and empty snacks with parental love. Real love for your children should encourage you to restrict refined sugars and refined flours, fats, artificial colorings and flavorings in an effort to improve their health in mind and body. Tell your children that the reason you don't want them to eat these extraneous foods is BECAUSE YOU LOVE THEM and you want them to be strong and healthy. They might not always like the answer but they will understand it and won't stop loving you.

If you are action-oriented, you may wish to join ACT (Action For Children's Television, 46 Austin Street, Newtonville, Mass. 02160—$5 membership fee includes a news letter). This non-profit group of parents and professionals are dedicated to better child oriented television without unnecessary and overly-sugared commercials.

Here are some snack ideas I'd like to share. Some are sugar-free, some are not. Most contain no salt. Recipes that do contain sugar have been selected because they include other nutritious ingredients which give them redeeming value. Honey, because of its cost, is not always a practical substitute for white sugar. Variety, not sugar or salt, is the spice of life. Much as I would prefer to live in a world free of refined sugar, my taste buds, my children, my family, my neighbors, my community and our schools make this virtually impossible. But I do work at it!

FROZEN SNACKS

The following popsicle recipes don't specify paper cup size or popsicle mold size. Only you know the amount your child can consume in one sitting with minimum drip.

FROZEN BANANAS
1 banana
2 popsicle sticks
Optional: honey and toasted wheat germ or chopped
nuts; peanut butter

Peel one firm, ripe banana. Cut in half, or even thirds. Insert one stick lengthwise through the center of each section. Wrap in plastic and place in the freezer. When ready to eat, dip in honey, (or smush with peanut butter) and roll in toasted wheat germ or chopped nuts, if using. These are good without being dipped in anything. (Yes, I know you can also dip them in melted chocolate chips, but why bother?)

ORANGE JUICE-SICLES
1 (6 oz.) can frozen orange juice
3 cans cold water
1 egg white
2 Tbsp. sweetener (sugar or honey)
popsicle sticks and cups

Mix in blender. Pour into molds, insert sticks and freeze.

VARIETY PACK POPSICLES
1 (6 oz.) can frozen orange juice concentrate, softened (or
   use grape juice, cranberry cocktail or Hawaiian Punch)
1 (6 oz.) can water
1 pt. vanilla ice cream, softened (or two containers of plain
   yogurt)
popsicle sticks and cups

Whir in a blender. Pour into molds, insert sticks, and freeze.

POLYNESIAN POPSICLES
1 cup skim milk
1 envelope unflavored gelatin
½ cup sugar or honey
1¼ cups apricot nectar or canned pineapple juice
1 egg white

popsicle sticks and cups

Pour milk into blender and add gelatin. Let soften for one minute before adding the rest of the ingredients to whip. Pour into molds, insert sticks and freeze.

CREAMSICLES
1 (16 oz.) can peaches in light syrup or 2 fresh ripe peaches,
   sliced and pitted
1 cup heavy cream
1 tsp. sugar or honey

Whip cream in a blender for 30-45 seconds. Add peaches and honey. Whir until smooth. Pour into molds, insert sticks and freeze.

CHOCOLATE POPS

1 (8 oz.) container plain yogurt
2 Tbsp. cocoa or carob powder
2 Tbsp. brown sugar or honey

Liquify in a blender, pour into molds, insert popsicle sticks and freeze.

SNOW CONES

Crush several ice cubes with ½ cup water in a blender, turning it on and off to achieve a snowy consistency. Pour over the "snow," which has been scooped into paper cups, either:

1) 2 Tbsp. thawed frozen juice or concentrate
or
2) 2 Tbsp. warmed honey to which food coloring has been added.

KEEP-ON-HAND SNOW CONES

Freeze orange juice (or any other flavored juice) in ice cube trays. Pop frozen juice cubes into a plastic bag to store. Put three to six of these cubes at a time in a blender. Turn blender on and off until cubes reach snowy consistency. Pile into a paper cup to serve.

The whole batch blended at once will keep its carnival consistency stored in a container in the freezer. Kids can serve themselves. Adding a little water makes it a "slush." Even kids who don't usually care for orange juice like it this way.

ONE LAST FREEZER IDEA: Offer your child a small paper cupful of frozen peas or frozen cut corn right from the package. For a change try freezing green grapes.

DIPPY SNACKS

With carrots, celery, green pepper strips, cucumber slices, cherry tomatoes, cauliflower pieces or crackers, try any of the following:

CHEESE SPREAD
 1 stick (½ cup) butter or margarine, softened
 1 cup cottage cheese
 garlic powder

Blend shortening with cottage cheese. A blender or baby food grinder will give you a smoother consistency than whipping with a fork. Add garlic powder to taste. Refrigerate in a covered container.

DIP IT AGAIN
 1 (8 oz.) container of plain yogurt.
 1 cup sour cream
 1 pkg. onion soup mix

Combine and chill before serving.

BETTER-WITH-BUTTERMILK DIP
 1 cup buttermilk
 2 cups mayonnaise
 1 cup sour cream (imitation is o.k.) or yogurt
 1 envelope Ranch style salad dressing mix

Stir together and chill. For use as salad dressing, substitute a second cup of buttermilk for the sour cream or yogurt.

HINT: Use cucumber "coins" in place of crackers.

Other quickie dippies that make up in small quantities are:
● Blend a ⅓ to a ½ mashed banana with 2 or 3 tsps. of mayonnaise.

● Whip together 1 tsp. of smooth peanut butter with 1 tsp. of mayonnaise. If still too thick, add a few drops of milk.

● Mix ½ tsp. of lemon juice and ½ tsp. of honey or sugar to 1 or 2 tsp. of mayonnaise.

CHERRY BALLS

Stuff whole (or half) cherry tomatoes with cream cheese, a cheese spread, egg salad or tuna salad.

Actually thinking of snacks as hors d'oeuvres — rather than desserts — will open up a whole new way of looking at this category.

CRUNCHY

Have you thought of putting crackers in your cookie jar? They are usually made with less sugar. You can fill a cookie jar with peanuts-in-the-shell. Or keep on hand a jar of nuts and raisins with a few chocolate chips thrown in. Campers call this mixture "Gorp."

POPCORN

Of all the gadgets available to us today the electric popper is probably one of the best you can buy from a nutritional snack point-of-view. Popcorn is good tasting, fun to make and a popular sugar-free food. It is low in calories, at least until you add coatings. It is also a good source of fiber. If you don't have a popcorn maker you can make do nicely with a large covered pot on the stove top using ¼ cup of oil to ½ cup of popping corn. Forget salt and try any of the following for a change of taste:

TOPPINGS: In addition to melted butter toppings try sprinkling grated Parmesan or American cheese on popcorn. Or mix with peanuts, or cinnamon.

Package extra popcorn in small plastic bags with twist ties; excellent for an out-of-doors treat, car ride or TV special snack.

HONEY "CRACKER JACKS" (my husband's favorite!)

> ½ cup (6 Tbsp.) honey
> ¼ cup butter or margarine
> 6 cups popped corn
> 1 cup shelled peanuts

(continued on next page)

Heat honey and shortening in a saucepan until blended. Cool. Pour over popcorn which has been mixed with peanuts, stirring as you pour. When well-coated, spread on a pan in a single layer. Bake at 350 degrees 5-10 minutes or until crisp, stirring several times. The difference between crisp (not brown) and burnt can be a matter of minutes. Package in plastic bags and twist-tie. If you want it to be mistaken for the "real thing" add a small toy.

Variation: Food coloring added to honey gives a festive appearance.

Commercial Cracker Jacks, though sugar-coated, contain no artificial colorings or flavorings and are mainly popcorn.

POPCORN CANDY CLUSTERS
1 cup (8 oz.) semi-sweet chocolate chips
1 cup freshly popped popcorn
1 cup nuts

Melt chocolate chips. Add popcorn and nuts and stir until they are well coated. Drop by spoonfuls onto a cookie sheet or wax paper and let set till firm. If the crowd is rushing you for a taste, chill the clusters in the freezer for 5 minutes. When firm, store in plastic bags.

CRUNCHO MIX
Mix:
4 cups crunchy cereal (Cheerios, Corn Chex, etc., or any combination)
1 cup peanuts or mixed nuts
1 cup pretzel sticks, the smallest size
1 cup seasoned croutons

Combine:
½ cup salad oil or 6 Tbsp. melted butter
2 tsp. Worcestershire Sauce
¼ tsp garlic powder

In a large shallow pan coat crunchy ingredients with the combined oil and seasonings. Heat in oven at 250 degrees for about 45 minutes, stirring every 15 minutes. Spread on absorbent paper to cool.

SWORDS

Banana slices, cheese slices, etc., can be "speared" on thin pretzel sticks.

UN-CANDY BARS

1 loaf of sliced bread, preferably whole wheat
1 pkg. peanuts, chopped
1 cup peanut butter,
peanut oil
Optional: ¼ cup toasted wheat germ

Trim crusts from bread. Halve slices. Dry bread and crusts on a cookie sheet overnight in your oven, or in the oven at 150 degrees for half an hour. Crumb dry crusts in a blender. Combine crust crumbs with chopped nuts and wheat germ, if using. Thin peanut butter with oil. Spread with, or dip the bread in, the thinned peanut butter, then roll it in the nut/crumb mixture. Store in an airtight container.

Variation: Add Tbsp. of cocoa or carob powder to the thinned peanut butter.

BREAKFAST GRANOLA BARS (They hold together well and are so-o-o easy!)

2 cups granola
2 eggs, beaten
Optional: Dash of vanilla for sweetening

Combine the granola and eggs in a greased 8" square pan. Bake at 350⁰ for 15 minutes. Cut into 8 bars. When serving spread with jam, honey or peanut butter.

Excellent served with a spread of peanut butter, honey or jam.

GRANOLA BARS

½ cup light corn syrup
⅔ cup (10 Tbsp.) peanut butter
3 cups granola, bought or homemade (page 94)
Optional: 1 carrot, grated

Butter a 9-inch square pan. In a 3-quart saucepan boil corn syrup for 1 minute only, stirring constantly. Remove from heat. Stir in peanut butter. Stir in granola, and grated carrot if using. Work fast as it hardens quickly. Transfer to pan. Spread and pat in place with a spoon or dampened spatula. Cool for an hour before cutting into bars.

GRAPE GRANOLA BARS

½ cup butterscotch chips
⅔ cup grape jelly
2 cups granola
1 cup oatmeal, uncooked
½ cup peanuts

Melt butterscotch chips over low heat, stirring constantly. Add jelly and stir till blended. Remove from heat. Add granola, oatmeal and chopped peanuts. Mix till well coated. Spread in a buttered 9-inch square pan. Refrigerate until firm. Cut into bars.

CRUNCHIES

½ cup butter or margarine
¼ cup (3 Tbsp.) honey
¼ cup sugar
4 cups oatmeal, uncooked
Optional: 1 cup raisins

Melt shortening. Add honey and sugar. Add oatmeal (and raisins) quickly before sugar dissolves completely. Blend well and press into a buttered 9 x 13 inch pan. Bake at 400 degrees for 8-10 minutes. Cut into squares while still slightly warm but don't remove from pan until they are firm.

Variation: Dribble ¾ cup or less of melted chocolate chips over Crunchies while they are still warm.

GREAT GORPIES! (A favorite to make and to eat!)

2 sticks (1 cup) butter or margarine
1 cup brown sugar
1 handful* each of   *adult — 1 handful
raisins   child — 2-3 handfuls
peanuts
chocolate chips
2 cups flour (white or half white, half whole wheat)
1 tsp. baking soda
2 tsp. milk

Cream shortening and sugar till smooth. Add all the handfuls going heavier on the first two and lighter on the chocolate chips. Mix well, then add combined flour and baking soda. Add milk. Drop by tablespoons on a greased cookie sheet. Bake at 350 degrees about 10 minutes or until done. Leave on cookie sheet a minute or two before lifting them off, as they might crumble. Makes 3 doz. cookies.

PEANUT BUTTER COOKIES
Cream together:
>   1 cup peanut butter
>   ½ cup (1 stick) butter or margarine
>   ½ cup brown sugar
>   ½ cup (6 Tbsp.) honey
>   1 egg, beaten

Combine and add:
>   2 ½ cups flour white or (half white, half whole wheat)
>   1 tsp. baking powder

Roll into little balls. Place on a greased cookie sheet and flatten with a fork which has been dipped in oil or water. Bake at 350 degrees for 15 minutes.

>   Optional: Add chocolate chips to dough.

QUICKIE COOKIES A LA STOVE TOP
>   1 cup sugar
>   2 Tbsp. cocoa or carob powder
>   ¼ cup (½ stick) butter or margarine
>   ¼ cup milk
>   ½ tsp. vanilla
>   ¼ cup (4 Tbsp.) peanut butter
>   1 ½ cups oatmeal, uncooked
>   ½ cup toasted wheat germ

Combine sugar, cocoa, butter and milk in a saucepan and boil over medium heat for 1 minute. Stirring constantly, fold in remaining ingredients. Drop with a teaspoon on wax paper and let harden. Work quickly because the hardening doesn't take long. Store in an airtight container because they can also dry out.

NO-BAKE DATE BALLS
>   ¾ cup brown sugar
>   2 eggs, beaten
>   1 cup dates, cut up
>   1 cup chopped nuts
>   2 cups cereal (1 cup each of any of the following: Rice Krispies, granola or a puffed cereal)

In a two-quart saucepan mix sugar, eggs and dates. Stir over medium heat about 5 minutes or until mixture pulls away from the pan. Cook 3 minutes longer. Remove from heat and add vanilla and nuts. Fold in cereal. Butter fingers to form mixture into balls. Let cool. Store in an airtight container.

>   Optional: Roll balls in coconut.

YUMMIE BALLS
Combine:
>½ cup (7 Tbsp.) peanut butter
>½ cup (6 Tbsp.) honey
>½ cup cocoa or carob powder
>1 cup toasted wheat germ
>1 cup peanuts or soy nuts (chopped if preferred)
>½ cup sunflower seeds

Roll into balls and roll in coconut. Refrigerate if using a refrigerated brand of peanut butter, which would be preferable.

JUST PLAIN GOOD

Magic Finger "Jell-O," the kind that disappears before your very eyes, is an all-time favorite of kids. If you want it without artificial flavorings and colorings, try the next recipe. If you want it without artificial flavorings and colorings and without SUGAR, try Apple Finger Jello.

GRAPE FINGER JELLO
>1 (12 oz.) can frozen grape juice concentrate, thawed
>3 envelopes unflavored gelatin
>1 ½ cups (1 can) water

Soften gelatin in grape juice. Boil the water, add the juice/gelatin mixture and stir till gelatin dissolves. Remove from heat, pour into a lightly greased 9 x 13-inch pan and chill. Cut into squares when firm. Refrigerate in a covered container.

>Variation: You can substitute frozen cranberry juice cocktail concentrate for grape juice.

>Note: This is a good lunch box and traveling fare. It can go unrefrigerated for 4 hours under normal conditions.

APPLE FINGER JELLO
>1 (12 oz.) can frozen apple (or pear/apple) juice concentrate, thawed
>3 envelopes unflavored gelatin
>1 ½ cups (1 can) water

Follow directions for Grape Finger Jello.

>Variation: By using only 2 envelopes of unflavored gelatin you can make regular apple jello.

If you have 2 bananas on hand, one fun way of serving this extra firm gelatin snack is as:

SLIPPERY CIRCLES

Let any of the above recipes for Finger "Jello" stand and chill till thickened, which doesn't take very long (15 minutes to 25 minutes). Place a spoonful of the gelatin into each of 4 empty and clean 6-oz. cans, such as usually used for frozen orange juice. Cut a peeled banana in half and center it in the can. Spoon in remaining gelatin. Chill till firm. To unmold, dip to rim in warm water and let it slide out. Or remove bottom of can if more appropriate. Cut in slices.

SUNSHINE SQUARES (A Finger "Jello" that is good even for breakfast.)

4 envelopes unflavored gelatin
¾ cup pineapple juice
1 cup boiling water
¼ cup sugar
1 cup orange juice

Soften gelatin in pineapple juice. Add to boiling water and stir until dissolved. Add sweetener and orange juice. Chill in a 9 x 9-inch pan, then cut in squares. Refrigerate in a covered container.

Variation: If you wish to use honey instead of sugar, decrease the orange juice by 1/8 of a cup.

APPLE RING SNACKS

Why pay for Weight Watcher's Apple Snack when you can make your own?

Peel an apple and remove the core. Slice in rings. Place on a lightly greased cookie sheet, or on clear plastic wrap laid out on a cookie sheet. Dry in an electric oven at low or warm temperature; in a gas oven the pilot light is sufficient. Drying takes 6-9 hours, making this a good overnight project. The size of the apple slices and your oven temperature are the variables you will have to experiment with. The apples need not be dried to a crisp. Store in an airtight container. These should last several weeks at room temperature. Good for traveling!

FRUIT LEATHER

Use apples, peaches, pears or nectarines to make this yummy dried "candy." The fruit can be the "too-hard-to-eat" variety or the "too-ripe-and-the-last-piece" variety. It even works on canned fruit which is well drained. Use mashed or pureed fruit. Two methods work well. FIRST is the blender way. Peel and core fruit, blend till smooth, then cook 5 minutes in a saucepan over moderate heat. SECOND is the freeze-defrost method. In advance, peel and core fruit and place it wrapped in the freezer. Remove from freezer an hour before using so it can start to defrost. Cook in a saucepan, mashing with fork as you go. Cook for 5-10 minutes. If very watery, drain. While cooking add 1 tsp. honey for each piece of fruit you are using. (Cook the different fruits separately, though you can cook 1 piece or a dozen of the same type at one time.)

Lay out clear plastic wrap (or cut open small plastic bags) on a cookie sheet or broiling tray. Use one piece for each piece of fruit you have cooked. Spoon mixture onto the wrap staying away from its edge. Spread as thin as possible. If you spread another piece of plastic wrap over the mixture and press down with a wide spatula, it helps to make it evenly thin. Be sure to remove this top sheet of plastic before drying.

Place your tray in the oven (at night, we suggest) which is turned on to its lowest possible heat or with just the pilot light on, and leave overnight (6-8 hrs.). The plastic wrap will not melt! If it is dry by breakfast, remove from the oven (if not, wait a while longer) and roll up the plastic wrap (with the dried fruit) as if it were a jelly roll.

THEN—PEEL AND EAT!

It will last several months this way—if your children don't discover it, that is. If you don't understand how this should look, stop in at a health food store and ask to look at their fruit roll, and the price of it!

"CANDIED" APPLE

        1 apple
        1 popsicle stick
        honey
        nuts and/or toasted wheat germ

Insert stick into the top of an apple. Dip the apple into a bowl of honey, coating evenly. Hold apple over bowl until excess honey has dripped off. (Don't rush this step.) Roll apple in chopped nuts or toasted wheat germ.

44

SOFT WHOLEWHEAT PRETZELS

    2 (16 oz.) loaves frozen whole wheat bread dough, thawed
    1 egg white, slightly beaten
    1 tsp. water
    coarse salt (optional)

Thaw bread in the refrigerator overnight. From each loaf shape 12 1-½ inch balls. Roll each ball into a rope approximately 14 inches long. Shape into pretzels by forming a knot and looping ends through. Arrange pretzels one inch apart on well-greased baking sheet. Let stand for 20 minutes. Brush combined egg white and water on pretzels, then sprinkle with coarse salt. Place a shallow pan containing one inch of boiling water on a lower rack in the oven. Bake pretzels on a cookie sheet on a rack above the water at 350 degrees for 20 minutes or till golden brown. Makes two dozen pretzels.

> Variation 1: Pretzel sticks can be made by beginning with balls rolled into 8 inch sticks. Try pretzel letters, which is something your children will enjoy helping you do.

> Variation 2: Roll sticks 4-6 inches long in a mixture of melted butter, cinnamon and sugar before baking.

SNACKING CAKE

    1 cup (2 sticks) butter or margarine, softened
    1-1/2 cups brown sugar
    1 cup cottage cheese
    2 eggs
    1 tsp. almond or vanilla flavoring
    2-1/2 cups flour (white or half white, half whole wheat)
    1/2 cup cocoa or carob powder
    1 tsp. baking soda
    1 tsp. baking powder
    2 cups oatmeal, uncooked
    Optional: 1/2 cup chopped nuts or sunflower seeds

Cream the butter or margarine with the sugar, using an electric mixer. Beat in cottage cheese. Add eggs, one at a time. Add flavoring. Combine dry ingredients, gradually add to creamed mixture, mixing well. Add nuts or seeds, if using. Bake in a greased and floured 9 x 11-inch pan at 350 degrees for 35 to 45 minutes or till done. You may wish to add a topping or frosting to the cake.

SNACK DRINKS

We tend to forget that the drinks we rely on to satisfy our thirst also provide many calories. Drinks, therefore, do qualify as snacks.

A "Best Bets" list of beverages:

Water
Orange Juice
Milk
Apple Juice (with no sugar added)
Grape Juice (in bottles there is no sugar added)
Fruit Nectars
Tomato Juice (and vegetable juices in general)
Artificially sweetened drinks

WATER

Yes, water is really our best beverage, though in all honesty I agree it does not qualify as a snack drink. It is the only drink on the list with no calories. In recent history it has lost popularity to its competitors but water does have a value beyond washing dishes and flushing toilets. Not only is it vital to our body functions, it is readily available and CHEAP. Remember that water has been the number one drink for thousands of years. Soda did not travel on covered wagons. If you want your water to seem more appetizing, keep it cold in a nice container in the refrigerator. A young child may be enticed to drink water from his or her own container, small enough for safe pouring, or from a jug with a spigot. Plastic cups in a lower drawer encourage self-help and can save you many "I'M THIRSTY" trips.

ORANGE JUICE

Orange juice is one of the best drinks we have to offer our families today because it is both inexpensive and naturally sweet. Don't just relegate orange juice to morning breakfast. It is a terrific drink all day long. The cost per serving for orange juice made from frozen concentrate is approximately 10 cents for an 8-ounce glass. (For the same quantity you are paying at least 16 cents for soda.) While Tang costs about as much per serving as frozen orange juice the label will inform you that you are offering your children sugar and a variety of chemicals instead of natural orange juice. It is also a good idea to supplement orange juice with oranges themselves. The pulp and the meat of the orange have important nutrients that are missing from frozen concentrate.

MILK

Milk is a terrific food—yes, FOOD. Most health spokesmen today recommend drinking skim milk from age two since we seem to get enough fats elsewhere in our diet. The only difference between skim milk and regular milk is the fat content. Milk provides a good supply of vitamins A and D which you might not be getting elsewhere in your diet. Milk is also a major source of protein as well as calcium for growing children. If your child has an aversion to milk, however, and even the addition of carob powder or cocoa won't change his/her mind, do not despair. Cheese, yogurt, cottage cheese and even quality ice cream are good substitutes. Dark greens are also a good source of calcium. Powdered milk is an excellent method for sneaking in extra milk value as it can be added to many foods including cookies, scrambled eggs, frostings, dips, and even milk itself. While this is a good enrichment idea, do not get carried away with it as your body will require extra liquids to make proper use of it. (It sort of reconstitutes internally.)

APPLE JUICE

Apple juice is available inexpensively year round if you buy it as frozen concentrate. It is available with no sugar added, and of course in the fall you can often find inexpensive jugs of it.

GRAPE JUICE

Bottled, this is a delicious, sugar-free drink (albeit expensive) which children enjoy. It can be stretched by adding water to it, adding lemon juice and some sweetener. The frozen variety does have sugar added but sugar is not the first ingredient on the label. (Frozen cranberry juice cocktail is also sugared but it has other good-for-you qualities.)

FRUIT NECTARS

Nectars are rich drinks, thicker than juices because they contain the fruit pulp. They can also be easily thinned with water or carbonated sodas. Most grocery-variety nectars contain added sugar.

Or make your own:

Apricot Nectar

½ cup dried apricots soaked in 2 cups of pineapple juice. Whir in blender till smooth.

TOMATO JUICE
Tomato juice and most other vegetable juices have the advantage of being low in calories and high in nutrients. The only problem seems to be that they are also universally low in acceptance by children.

ARTIFICIALLY SWEETENED DRINKS
Diet pop, while not the perfect drink, is somewhat better than the regular soft drinks you might find your family drinking in quantity. A regular can of soda (12 oz.) has approximately 9-10 tsps. of sugar added. While diet soda does cut back on this high sugar intake, you are still downing a lot of saccharin as well as artificial flavorings and colorings. We ingest practically all of our saccharin from these diet sodas. Think of diet sodas as treats and not staples. Artificially sweetened instant diet iced tea is an inexpensive sweet drink that can be watered down and still be tasty.

Studies are indicating that saccharin in large amounts may be a health hazard. Since quantity is a factor it would seem to be best to err on the side of less versus more.

You and your family may not find all the drinks on the above list acceptable. Cross out those that won't work for you and keep the rest of the list on hand, or try:

DO-IT-YOURSELF SODA POP
Apple soda
Combine one container of frozen unsweetened apple juice with any carbonated soda. By using the carbonated drink to reconstitute the apple juice you provide a delightful bubbly drink resembling pop.

Fruit fizz
Combine carbonated water with fruit juice or nectar in equal amounts. For a lighter drink, add more soda; for a heavier drink, add more juice; for a sweeter drink, add honey.

PARADISE PUNCH
1 cup low calorie tropical fruit flavored drink
1 banana
2 Tbsp. powdered milk
Blend and serve.

ORANGE FROTH (This is a good afternoon drink that will serve the whole block!)

3 cups water
1 (6 oz.) can frozen orange juice concentrate, thawed
1 cup powdered dry milk
Optional: nutmeg, coconut powder, raw egg or banana

Whip ingredients together in a blender and serve.

FROZEN FRUIT SLUSH

1 can of fruit, frozen

Defrost slightly by holding can under hot running tap water for a minute or two. Open can and put contents into your blender. If the can is large, use only one or two cups of the frozen fruit. Blend to slush consistency and serve in a glass with a straw.

HINT: Try to use fruits packed in light or natural syrup to avoid unnecessary sugar.

FRUIT SLURP

1 cup milk, ice milk, ice cream or plain yogurt
1 banana
1 peach or nectarine
a handful of strawberries

Actually you can use a combination of fresh fruits. Sweeten with honey, whip in a blender and then drink. If too thick, add ½ cup milk. This makes an excellent bedtime snack.

BANANA SMOOTHY

1 ½ cups milk
1 large banana
1 Tbsp. honey
¼ tsp. vanilla

Combine in a blender and mix well. You can also use a frozen banana. (Freezing is a good way to use up extra or left-over bananas.)

FROZEN YOGURT SHAKE

1 cup plain yogurt
1 cup ice cream or frozen yogurt
½ cup milk
½ cup fruit plus 1 Tbsp. jam (such as strawberries and strawberry jam)

Whir in a blender and enjoy.

Variation: A larger amount of fruit or frozen fruit would eliminate need for jam.

49

CHOCOLATE AND CAROB

Chocolate as we know it is a bitter substance when eaten by itself but is made more palatable by the addition of a lot of sugar. Cocoa powdered drink is chocolate plus sugar. As all teenagers with blemishes know, chocolate has a very high fat content—52 percent in fact. Chocolate also contains a goodly amount of caffeine. (Caffeine is a stimulant that affects the nervous system as well as the basic endocrine system which provides for growth and metabolism.) We don't serve our children coffee or tea because of our concern over caffeine, yet somehow chocolate treats are acceptable. (Cola beverages and Dr. Pepper also contain caffeine.)

	milligrams of caffeine per 8-oz. serving
regular coffee	100-150
instant coffee	85
decafeinated coffee	3
tea	50
1 oz. chocolate bar	20
cola drinks	20-40
low calorie lemon instant tea	25

Is there an option? Fortunately, yes. It is called carob and it is a naturally sweet substance with a taste very similar to chocolate. I resisted trying carob for a long time—another one of those "health foods"—even though I knew its fat content was low (2 percent), it had no caffeine (what child needs extra stimulation), and that it was high in natural sugars and low in starch. Carob is sold in health food stores, food co-ops and in grocery stores with specialty food sections.

There is carob powder and carob drink. In the latter, carob is combined with brown sugar to enhance its taste. When I finally tried carob I started with the drink. I did not mention it to my children, I simply gave it to them as I would a glass of chocolate milk with their lunch while they watched Sesame Street (naturally!). To my surprise, they never said a word to me about the taste or suggested that it tasted different. Depending on where or how it's used carob can have a slightly raw taste or after taste. Some people recommend adding a pinch of instant coffee or using carob in vegetable oil base recipes to avoid this. Mixing one-half carob and one-half cocoa is a good way to start. In a health food store or co-op, you can also find carob chips to use in baking. Carob is worth experimenting with.

COLD "C" DRINK
¾ cup milk
¼ cup cocoa or carob drink or carob powder
2 tsp. honey
1 ice cube
Whir in blender.

HOT INSTANT "C" MIX
8 cups powdered dry milk
¾ cup sugar
1 cup cocoa or carob drink or carob powder
1 tsp. cinnamon
1 (6 oz.) jar of coffee creamer
Mix together well and store in a container with tight-fitting lid. To serve, simply stir ⅓ cup of this mixture in a mug of boiling water.

One last word on behalf of the dental community:

It has been shown that frequent eating causes more cavities unless you really do brush and floss after every meal and snack. This is especially true when foods are sugared or sticky. Unfortunately this edict applies to honey and raisins as well as to candy and cake..All the snacks described herein will not make the recommended lists of all dentists.

You can please some of the nutritionists, doctors and dentists some of the time—but not all of them all of the time.

It's Delicious . . . It's (more) Nutritious . . . It's Dessert

If I could choose one word in our vocabulary to lose, dessert would be it. Years ago when a sweet was a treat rather than an hourly occurrence, dessert was the luxurious finish to a meal. Today we get as much sugar along with our meals (i.e., breakfast cereals, soft drinks, etc.) as in dessert.

My all time favorite dessert recipe is:

"NOTTO HAVEONE"
    0 cups flour
    0 cups sugar
    0 tsp. salt
        no dash of anything
Easy to make, inexpensive and non-fattening, no dishes to clean and second helpings are never a problem.

If you prefer a dessert with more taste and texture, the next consideration would be fruit, cheese and crackers, or all three. Or maybe a large bowl of unshelled nuts served with nutcrackers and toothpicks.

"But my husband would feel denied," you claim. Or, "My children would threaten to move in with the neighbors" (now there's an appealing idea!) However, if you are going to cut back on the 100 plus pounds of refined sugar consumed per person each year in your family, this is obviously the place to start.

Perhaps the enormity of all this excess sugar consumption has already hit home if you have one or more overweight children. The easiest and fastest way to achieve obesity is with excess sugar. Early fat can determine the number of fat cells we carry into adulthood, making obesity an almost inescapable problem. While the best remedy for excess weight is regular exercise, the second best is to cut back on refined sugar consumption and the third best is to cut back on refined flour consumption.

Less (sugar) is better, so here are some ideas to help make a dent in your sugar consumption. A few of the recipes have more sugar than I like to use but at least these recipes have other ingredients to give them some "redeeming value." In other words, if you persist in the sweetened route, at least get something for your money...I mean, your body.

JUNKET (Pudding you can make without artificial colorings and flavorings)
  2 cups milk
  ⅔ cup powdered milk
  ¼ cup white or brown sugar or 2 Tbsp. honey
  1 tsp. vanilla
  1 rennet tablet
Combine milk, powdered milk and sweetener in a saucepan. Heat until lukewarm, 110 degrees. Temperature is very important. Meanwhile dissolve rennet tablet in 1 Tbsp. of water and stir into warm milk no longer than 10 *seconds*. Pour into custard cups. DO NOT MOVE CUPS UNTIL JUNKET IS SET, which takes about 10 minutes.

Rennet tablets, if not found next to the unflavored gelatin envelopes in your grocery store, may be found in drugstores. They are quite inexpensive.

Variation: Sweeten to taste with molasses instead of sugar or honey. Omit vanilla and flavor to taste with almond extract or freshly shredded orange rind or lemon rind.
Before adding rennet tablet, stir into milk ½ cup of graham cracker crumbs or toasted wheat germ or Grape Nuts. Add a sprinkle of cinnamon.

KEEP-ON-HAND PUDDING MIX (Not as fast or as firm as the commercial variety, but very good.)

2 ¾ cups powdered milk
1½ cups sugar
½ cup cornstarch
1 tsp. salt

Blend these four ingredients well and store in an airtight container.

To make Vanilla Pudding

1 cup milk
½ cup water
¾ cup of pudding mix combined with a ½ cup water
1 beaten egg
1/ tsp. vanilla flavoring

Heat milk mixed with water. Stir pudding blended with water into hot milk. Cook over a medium heat, stirring constantly, until it boils and thickens. Boil for 1 minute. Remove from heat and add in beaten egg and flavoring. Let cool and chill. Makes 4 to 6 servings.

To make Chocolate Pudding

Prepare as for Vanilla Pudding but add ¼ cup cocoa or carob to the ¾ cup of pudding mix used.

BANANA CUSTARD (This tastes like banana cream pie but without a crust.)

3 egg yolks
1 whole egg
1 ½ cups milk
½ cup sugar
¼ cup flour
1 tsp. vanilla
3 egg whites
¼ tsp. cream of tartar
4 Tbsp. sugar
1 large banana

In a heavy saucepan beat egg yolks and the one whole egg. Add milk and the combined sugar and flour. Stir continuously over low heat until mixture thickens. Remove from heat, add vanilla and let cool. Now beat egg whites with cream of tartar till frothy. Add remaining sugar and continue beating till egg whites form stiff peaks. Pour half of the custard mixture evenly divided among six custard cups. Evenly distribute sliced banana over custard. Pour remaining custard into cups. Spoon egg white mixture over custard, sealing to edges of cups. Bake at 350 degrees for 10 minutes, about the time it takes to brown on top.

FROSTY CRANBERRY CUPCAKES

1 cup sour cream
¼ cup powdered sugar
1 (16 oz) can whole cranberry sauce
1 (8 oz) can crushed pineapple, undrained

Combine sour cream with powdered sugar. Stir in cranberry sauce and pineapple with liquid. Pour into cupcake liners, or into 9 x 13-inch pan for bars. Freeze. Remove from freezer 10 minutes before serving.

Variation: Use frozen strawberries instead of cranberry sauce.

FROZEN YOGURT

(Soft frozen yogurt stands are popping up all over the country. Why not try your hand at it?)

1 (8 oz.) container of plain yogurt.
1 cup of strawberries, blueberries or banana slices
Optional: Sweeten to taste

(continued on next page)

Whip this mixture in your blender. Put blender container into freezer for ½ hour. Remove and blend again. Repeat once or twice more, then pour into bowl or popsicle molds. If you don't have a blender, use a mixer.

Variation: Canned fruit also works well, especially pineapple. Also, serve frozen yogurt—frozen or simply refrigerated till firm—in ice cream cones.

JELL-YO
    1 (6 oz.) can frozen juice concentrate, thawed
    1 envelope unflavored gelatin
    1 cup water
    1/2 cup sugar or corn syrup
    1 (8 oz.) container of plain yogurt.
Soften gelatin in juice. In a saucepan, heat water to boiling, add gelatin/juice mixture, and sugar. Stir till dissolved. Remove from heat, cool for 5 minutes, add yogurt and mix well. Pour into bowl or individual dishes. Refrigerate till set.

Variation: Add contents of 1 small package of Jell-O to 1 cup of water. Heat to boiling. Cool and add plain yogurt. Let set in refrigerator.

FORTUNE COOKIES (This is a unique treat that can be made for or with children)
    1/4 cup flour
    2 Tbsp. brown sugar
    1 Tbsp. corn starch
      a dash of salt
    2 Tbsp. cooking oil
    1 egg white, beaten till stiff
    1/4 tsp. vanilla or lemon flavoring
    3 Tbsp. water
    8 to 10 paper "fortune" strips, either typed out or cut from magazines.
Combine flour, sugar, cornstarch and salt. Stir in oil and fold in egg white until mixture is smooth. Add flavoring and water and mix well. In a small skillet, an electric fry pan (medium heat) or on a lightly greased griddle, pour one tablespoon of batter, spreading it to a 3-inch circle. Cook for 4 minutes or till lightly browned, turn with a spatula and cook for one more minute. Batter will turn from beige to brown. Remove from grid-

(continued on next page)

dle and quickly place "fortune" paper in the center of the circle. Fold in half over the edge of a glass, and then in half again. Hold for a few seconds until cool, then place in an empty egg carton to help cookie keep its shape. These get better with practice. This recipe makes 8-10 fortune cookies. If they do not seem crisp enough for you, toast them in the oven at 300 degrees for 10 minutes, or just let them "sit around" a few days.

DANISH TURNOVERS
    2 oz. (1/2 cup) cottage cheese
    1/8 tsp. cinnamon
    1/8 tsp. vanilla
    1 Tbsp. sugar or honey
    1 pkg. refrigerated crescent rolls
Thoroughly combine first four ingredients. Use as filler for crescent rolls, then fold to form "Danish pastry" triangles. Bake at 375 degrees till rolls are browned.

Variation: Spoon filling on whole wheat toast. Heat in
        oven or toaster oven until bubbly.

PEANUT BUTTER FONDUE (Fun as well as good tasting!)
    1 cup creamy peanut butter
    1 cup light cream
    1/2 cup (6 Tbsp.) honey
    apple wedges
    peach quarters
    pear quarters
    banana chunks
    pitted dates
    fresh whole strawberries
    flaked coconut and/or toasted wheat germ
Place peanut butter in fondue pot. Gradually stir in cream and honey. Place over low heat, stirring constantly until mixture starts to boil. Keep warm on the table while serving. Spear fruit on fondue fork and dip into peanut butter mixture. Coat with coconut and/or toasted wheat germ if you wish.

SUPER FRIDGE FUDGE

1/2 cup (6 Tbsp.) honey
1/2 cup (7 Tbsp.) peanut butter
1/2 cup cocoa powder or carob
2 cups total, any combination of sesame seeds, sunflower seeds and chopped nuts
1/2 cup raisins or dates
1/2-1 cup shredded coconut

Heat honey and peanut butter. Quickly add cocoa powder or carob and stir. Remove from heat. Add seeds, nuts, coconut and dried fruit. Pour into a square, greased pan and refrigerate to harden. Cut in squares. Keep stored in refrigerator.

BETTER-FOR-YOU BROWNIES

1/4 cup oil
1 Tbsp. molasses
1 cup brown sugar
2 tsp. vanilla
2 eggs
1/2 cup broken pecans or walnuts
1 cup wheat germ
2/3 cup powdered milk
1/2 tsp. baking powder
1/4 cup cocoa powder or carob
or
2 sq. unsweetened baking chocolate

Mix together all ingredients except dry milk, baking powder and cocoa or carob powder. If using squares of chocolate, melt in a double boiler and add at this point. Combine dry milk, baking powder and carob. Stir into wet ingredients. Spread in a heavily greased 8 x 8-inch pan and bake at 350 degrees for approximately 30 minutes. Turn out of pan and cut into bars while still warm.

Optional: Sprinkle with powdered sugar.

CRANBERRY SQUARES

1 cup (2 sticks) butter or margarine
1 cup brown sugar
1 cup flour (white or half white, half whole wheat)
2 1/2 cups oatmeal, uncooked
1 (16 oz.) can whole cranberry sauce or 2 cups of homemade cranberry sauce
Optional: 1/2 cup toasted wheat germ

(continued on next page)

Mix butter, brown sugar, flour, oatmeal (and wheat germ) together. Work with fingers until mixture is in crumbs the size of peas. Pat half the mixture into an 8-inch pan. Spread cranberry sauce over it and top with remainder of mixture. Pat down gently. Bake at 375 degrees for 30 minutes or till lightly browned. Cut into squares while still warm.

EASY APPLE CRISP
4-6 apples, peeled, cored and sliced
1 Tbsp. lemon juice
1 cup oatmeal, uncooked
1/3 cup flour (white or whole wheat)
1/3 cup packed brown sugar
1 tsp. cinnamon
1/3 cup melted butter or margarine
Optional: 1/4 cup toasted wheat germ

Place apple slices in a greased 9-inch baking pan. Sprinkle with lemon juice. Combine dry ingredients and mix in melted butter until mixture is crumbly. Sprinkle over apples. Bake at 375 degrees until apples are tender (20-30 minutes). Serve warm or cold. Optional toppings are milk, cream or ice cream.

Hint: In the fall when apples are in season and you can't face another jar of apple sauce, buy some small aluminum pans and cook up several Easy Apple Crisps to put in the freezer.

PEACH CRUMBLE
1 (29 oz.) can* sliced cling peaches, drained
2 Tbsp. lemon juice
1/4 tsp. cinnamon
1 Tbsp. butter or margarine
1/4 cup melted shortening
1/3 cup brown sugar
1/3 cup flour (white or half white, half whole wheat)
1/4 tsp. baking soda
2/3 cup oatmeal, uncooked
1/2 tsp. vanilla
Optional: ice cream or cream or milk

Arrange peaches in buttered shallow 1 quart baking dish. Sprinkle with lemon juice and cinnamon. Dot with butter. Combine shortening and sugar in a bowl. Add rest of ingredients. Crumble with fingers and sprinkle on peaches. Bake at 350 degrees for 45 minutes. Makes four servings. Top with ice cream or cream or milk when ready to serve.

*peaches canned in water would be preferable.

60

RAISIN-NUT BARS

1/2 cup (1 stick) butter or margarine, melted
1/3 cup sugar
1/3 cup packed brown sugar
1/4 cup applesauce
1 egg
1 tsp. vanilla
1 cup flour (whole wheat or white)
1 tsp. baking powder
1/2 tsp. cinnamon
1/2 cup (or more) raisins
1/2 cup (or more) chopped nuts

Combine melted butter or margarine with sugars, applesauce, egg and vanilla. Combine flour, baking powder and cinnamon. Blend wet and dry mixtures then add in raisins and nuts. Bake in a greased 9-inch square pan for 30 minutes at 350 degrees. Let cool before cutting into bars.

CHEESE CAKE BARS (Fattening but delicious! How I envy those kids with all that energy to burn so that fat doesn't go to their hips as it does to mine.)

1 cup flour (white or half white, half whole wheat)
1/3 cup brown sugar, packed
6 Tbsp. butter or margarine, softened
1 (8 oz.) pkg. cream cheese, softened
1/4 cup sugar
1 egg
2 Tbsp. milk
2 Tbsp. lemon juice
1/2 tsp. vanilla
2 Tbsp. chopped walnuts
2 Tbsp. toasted wheat germ
2 Tbsp. oatmeal, uncooked

In a large mixing bowl combine flour and brown sugar. Cut in butter till mixture forms fine crumbs. Reserve 1 cup crumbs for topping. Press remainder into bottom of an ungreased 8-inch square pan. Bake in oven at 350 degrees for 15 minutes or till lightly browned. With a mixer, cream together cream cheese and sugar. Then add egg, milk, lemon juice and vanilla. Beat well. Spread batter on baked crust. Combine walnuts, crumb mixture, wheat germ and oatmeal and sprinkle over all. Bake at 350 degrees for 20-25 minutes. Cool and cut into squares.

DATE BARS

    1-1/4 cup pitted dates
    1/3 cup sugar
    1/2 cup water

Combine these ingredients in a saucepan and cook over a medium heat. Stir to mash the dates. When uniformly soft, remove from heat and cool.

    3/4 cup butter or margarine
    3/4 cup brown sugar
    1 cup flour (white or whole wheat)
    2 cups oatmeal
    1 tsp. baking soda

Blend these five ingredients well and press half of the mixture into the bottom of a greased and floured 8 to 9-inch square pan. Spread date mixture over the pressed crumb mixture. Top with remainder of the dry ingredients. Bake at 350 degrees for 45 minutes or till top is browned.

MELT-AWAY COOKIES

    1 cup (2 sticks) butter or margarine
    1/4 cup (3 Tbsp.) honey
    2 cups flour
    2 tsp. vanilla
    3/4 cup chopped nuts
    Optional: powdered sugar

Cream shortening and honey. Add flour, vanilla and nuts. Shape into 1/2 inch balls and flatten slightly with a fork. Bake on a lightly greased cookie sheet at 350 degrees for 10-12 minutes.

Optional: Dip in confectioners sugar.

COTTAGE CHEESE COOKIES

    1 cup (2 sticks) butter or margarine, softened
    1 cup creamed cottage cheese, small curd
    2 cups flour (white or half white, half whole wheat)
    strawberry preserves or any other filling

Cream together butter and cottage cheese. Work in flour and wrap dough in waxed paper. Place in refrigerator to harden. When cold, roll in thin sheets and cut into 3-inch squares and place on a lightly greased cookie sheet. Place a teaspoon of preserves (or honey) in center of each square and fold into a triangle, pressing edges together very firmly. Bake in preheated 350 degree oven for 15 minutes or until crust is brown and crisp.

These recipes can be used to make:

COLOSSAL COOKIES!

CRUNCHY CHOCOLATEY COOKIES
1 cup flour (white or half white/half whole wheat)
3 Tbsp. cocoa or carob
1/4 tsp. baking soda
1/2 tsp. baking powder
1/2 cup sugar or 3/4 cup honey
1/2 cup (1 stick) butter or margarine
1 egg

Combine flour, cocoa (or carob), baking soda and baking powder and mix well. Then combine softened butter or margarine, sweetener, vanilla and egg. Combine wet and dry ingredients together and mix well.

For Colossal Cookies, use 1/3 cup of dough per cookie. Follow directions at the top of the next page. Makes 4-6 cookies.

OATMEAL-RAISIN COOKIES
1 cup (2 sticks) butter or margarine
1-1/2 cups brown sugar
2 eggs, beaten
1 tsp. vanilla
2 cups flour (white, whole wheat or half and half)
2 1/3 cups oatmeal, uncooked
2 tsp. baking soda
1 tsp. cinnamon
1-1/2 cup raisins

Cream butter, sugar and then add eggs and vanilla. Separately combine dry ingredients then mix well with creamed mixture. Add raisins.

For Colossal Cookies, use 1/2 cup of dough per cookie. Follow directions at the top of the next page. Makes 10-12 cookies.

CHOCOLATE CHIP COOKIES
The unbeatable best of chocolate chip cookies recipes is the Original Toll House Cookie recipe found on the back of Nestle's semi-sweet chocolate morsels bag. It can be altered slightly— without loss of taste—by not using the salt called for; by using the Cornell Triple Rich Formula (see page 123); and by not using the whole 12-oz. bag of chocolate morsels.

For Colossal Cookies, use 1/2 cup of dough per cookie. Follow directions at the top of the next page. Makes 8-10 terrific cookies.

To Make Colossal Cookies:

Spoon dough onto a greased cookie sheet. Start out with not more than two at a time till you judge how much they spread and how big you want them. Lightly grease the bottom of a pie pan. Dip it into flour or sugar and use it to flatten each cookie into a 5-6 inch circle. Make sure each cookie is at least 2 inches from the edge. Baking time is 12-15 minutes at 350 degrees.

To seal each cookie in plastic wrap:

Wrap each cookie in a piece of clear plastic sufficent to completely cover cookie. Put a piece of brown heavy paper on a cookie sheet. Place wrapped cookies (as many as fit without overlapping) on the brown paper and put in 325 degree oven for 30 seconds until plastic shrinks tightly over the cookie. Remove and cool. Store sealed for a week or freeze for longer storage.

NOTE: These recipes may also be used to produce ordinary size cookies!

COOKIE CLUSTERS

2 squares white bark
1/2 cup (7 Tbsp.) peanut butter
4 cups granola
4 cups chow mein noodles

Melt the 2 squares of white bark in a 200 degree oven for 20 minutes in a 12x9x2-inch pan. Remove from the oven when completely softened and add peanut butter and mix well. In a bowl combine granola and noodles. Add this mixture to melted bark and peanut butter. Toss and coat mixture evenly. Drop by the tablespoon onto aluminum foil or wax paper. These cookies harden upon cooling completely. Makes 4 dozen.

WHIPPED CREAM GRAHAM CAKE (A good make-ahead treat!)

1 pint (2 cups) heavy cream
2 Tbsp. honey or sugar
32 squares (16 rectangles) of graham crackers

Beat cream with sweetner until stiff. Spread whipped cream heavily on one square and place it on a platter. Spread cream heavily on a second square and place it on top of the first. Continue until there is a stack of 4 squares. Press down gently on the top square so the cream squeezes out of the sides. Spread the excess along the sides. Repeat this procedure until there are

(continued on next page)

eight stacks. Slide them together till sides touch to form a rectangular cake of 2 squares by 4 squares. Use extra whipped cream to smooth over all the tops. Refrigerate. Allowing it to chill several hours before serving enables the crackers to soften. A dash of sprinkles over the top adds a party flavor without adding much additional sugar. Serves 8.

UNBIRTHDAY CAKE (A chocolatey treat which will make any day special; moist — heavy — delicious)

4 eggs, separated
1 cup sugar
1/2 cup (6 Tbsp.) honey
1 cup whole wheat flour
1 1/2 cups white flour
4 Tbsp. cocoa powder or carob
2 tsp. baking soda
2 cups sour cream
1 tsp. vanilla

Beat egg whites till frothy, add yolks and beat again. Add sweeteners and whole wheat flour. Mix well. Add cocoa & baking soda to white flour and stir into mixture alternately with sour cream. Stir in vanilla. Bake in a greased, floured bundt pan at 350 degrees for 50 minutes. Equally delectable baked in two greased and floured 9-inch pans or a large rectangular pan (30 minutes) or in 24 cupcake holders (20 minutes).

CARROT CAKE or Uncle Wiggly's Delight

1 cup oil
2 1/2 cups grated carrots (approximately 3 large carrots)
1 1/4 cups brown sugar
1/4 cup honey
4 eggs, beaten
2 tsp. baking soda
2 cups flour (white or half white, half whole wheat)
2 tsp. cinnamon

Combine first five ingredients and mix well. Add combined soda, flour and cinnamon. Bake in a greased and floured 13 x 9-inch pan at 325 degrees for 40-45 minutes. Cream cheese frosting (page 69) is the topping recommended here.

HINT: Defrost a 20 oz. bag of frozen cut carrots. Chop one cup at a time in a blender. Use whole amount as called for in above recipe.

ZUCCHINI BREAD (It tastes a lot better than it sounds!)
>2 1/2 cups flour (white or half white, half whole wheat)
>1/4 cup powdered milk
>1/2 cup wheat germ
>2 tsp. baking soda
>1/2 tsp. baking powder
>2 cups sugar (1 brown, 1 white)
>3 tsp. cinnamon
>1/2 tsp. nutmeg
>1 cup oil
>3 eggs, beaten
>3 tsp. vanilla
>1. cup chopped nuts
>2 cups (3 medium size) zucchini, with peel, grated

Combine above ingredients and bake in a well greased loaf pan at 350 degrees for one hour. This recipe makes two loaves.

>HINT: To grate zucchini quickly, place zucchini cut into chunks in a blender. Cover with water and blend at "CHOP" for a few seconds till processed. Drain off water and use.

LITTLE-BIT-OF-CHOCOLATE BARS (A small amount of chocolate goes a long way to help down these delicious—albeit slightly dry—bars.)
>1/2 cup (1 stick) butter or margarine
>1/2 cup brown sugar, packed
>1 tsp. vanilla
>1 egg
>1 1/2 cups flour (white or half white, half whole wheat)
>1 cup regular wheat germ
>1/2 cup semi-sweet chocolate chips

Cream butter and brown sugar in a large bowl. Beat in vanilla and egg. Stir in flour and wheat germ. Press evenly into an 8-inch square baking pan. Bake at 325 degrees for 20 minutes or till lightly browned. Remove from oven and immediately sprinkle top with chocolate chips. When the chocolate has softened, use a spatula or broad knife to spread it carefully over the top surface. Cool before cutting into bars. To store, separate layers with foil.

BANANA BREAD

1/4 cup butter or margarine
1/2 cup brown sugar
1 egg, beaten
1 cup bran cereal or uncooked oatmeal
4-5 mashed ripe bananas (about 1 1/2 cups)
1 tsp. vanilla
1 1/2 cups flour (white, whole wheat or a combination)
2 tsp. baking powder
1/2 tsp. baking soda
1/2 cup chopped nuts

Cream shortening and sugar until light. Add egg and mix. Then add the cereal, bananas and vanilla. Stir. Combine the remaining ingredients in a bowl and add to the first mixture, stirring only long enough to moisten the flour. Bake in a greased loaf pan at 350 degrees for an hour or until bread tests as done.

APPLESAUCE CAKE

2/3 cup margarine, melted
1 1/2 cups unsweetened applesauce — **hot**
1 cup sugar (less than 1 cup if using sweetened applesauce)
2 cups flour (white or half white, and half whole wheat)
2 tsp. baking soda
1 heaping tsp. cinnamon
1 cup raisins
Optional: 1 cup nuts
         2 Tbsp. wheat germ

Pour melted shortening into **hot** applesauce. Add sugar. Sift in flour, baking soda and cinnamon. Add raisins, nuts and wheat germ. Bake in a greased 9 x 13-inch pan at 375 degrees for 1 hour or in two 8-inch pans for 25 minutes and have one to freeze. Good while still warm topped with powdered sugar or whipped cream.

HINT: When cutting cake, let one child cut and the other have the first choice. You'll be delighted at how fairly this works.

WHOLESOME POUNDCAKE

     1 cup (2 sticks) butter or margarine
     2 cups packed brown sugar
     2 tsp. flavoring, vanilla or almond
     3 eggs
     2 cups flour (white, whole wheat or half and half)
     1/4 cup raw wheat germ
     1/2 tsp. baking soda
     1 cup plain yogurt
     Optional: 1/2 cup nuts or granola

With an electric mixer, beat together butter and brown sugar. Add in flavorings and eggs and beat till smooth. Combine flour, wheat germ and soda in a bowl and mix. Add flour mixture alternately with yogurt to batter, blending well after each addition. Bake at 325 degrees in two greased and floured loaf pans or one tube pan for about one hour. Cool for 1/2 hour before removing from the pans.

The unused balance of cookie and cake desserts can be stored in the freezer. Cakes are best sliced and wrapped individually for freezing. This method reduces the possibility that one member of the family will polish off any left out leftovers.

FROSTINGS

It's not hard to make your own frostings. They are so superior in taste and quality to any form of commercial mix that once you have found one or two favorites you won't want to settle for second best. Good-for-you frostings work fine on muffins and breads as well as on cookies and cakes.

WHIPPED CREAM

Whipped cream contains no chemicals and can be prepared from scratch very quickly. You can flavor it yourself.

     1 pint heavy **or** whipping cream
     2 tsp. honey or sugar

In a bowl combine cream and sweetener. Whip with an electric mixer or egg beater until mix is fluffy and holds its shape.

Variation: Whip cream nearly stiff. Add 1/2 cup powdered milk and whip 30 seconds. Dissolve 1
envelope of unflavored gelatin in 1 Tbsp. of
cold water, then heat till clear. Add to the
half whipped cream and finish whipping.
Cream will hold its shape nicely.

CREAM CHEESE FROSTING

3 oz. cream cheese
1/3 cup butter or margarine, softened
1 tsp. vanilla
1 1/2 cups powdered sugar
Optional: toasted wheat germ or chopped nuts

Whip together cream cheese and butter. Add vanilla and
powdered sugar. If too stiff for spreading, thin with a little milk.
Sprinkle with a nutty topping, if desired.

Variation: 8 oz. cream cheese
2 Tbsp. honey
1/4 cup heavy cream whipped till fluffy

Combine cream cheese and honey. Mix with whipped cream.

YOU'VE-GOT-CHOCOLATE-
ON-MY-PEANUT-BUTTER FROSTING

1/2 cup (7 Tbsp.) peanut butter
1 (6 oz.) pkg. chocolate chips

Melt peanut butter and chocolate chips together over medium heat until smooth and spreadable.

PEANUT BUTTER FROSTING

Combine:

1 cup powdered sugar
1/4 cup cream cheese
1/4 cup powdered milk
1/2 cup peanut butter
1/4 cup milk

Mix till smooth and then spread.

GOOD 'N EASY FROSTINGS

BASE: Cream together

> 2 Tbsp. butter or margarine,
> softened (or peanut butter)
> 1/4 cup (3 Tbsp.) honey
> 1 tsp. vanilla

FLAVORINGS: Add these to base and blend till smooth

Banana

> 2-3 Tbsp. milk, buttermilk or yogurt
> 1 cup powdered milk
> 1 mashed banana
> dash of cinnamon

Chocolate or Carob

> 2-3 Tbsp. milk, buttermilk or yogurt
> 1/4 cup cocoa or carob powder
> 2/3 cup powdered milk

Fruity

> 2-3 Tbsp. fruit juice
> 1 cup powdered milk
> grated orange or lemon rind

BROWN SUGAR FROSTING

Blend together:

> 3 Tbsp. butter or margarine, softened
> 1 1/2 cups brown sugar
> 1/2 cup canned evaporated milk
> 1 tsp. maple or vanilla flavorings
> 1/2 cup or more of powdered milk

NUTTY TOPPING

> 1/2 cup maple syrup
> 4 oz. walnuts, pecans, Brazil nuts or filberts

Pulverize nuts in a blender. Mix with syrup to a paste. Spread!

If you are still using the powdered sugar-plus-abit-of water combination for an icing, keep in mind that the liquid used can also be orange juice, lemon juice, yogurt, etc.

To Decorate

Any frosting can be squeezed from a small plastic bag with one corner cut out.

For natural frosting or icing colorings, add a bit of cranberry juice for pink; carrot juice for yellow/orange; grape juice concentrate for a dark pink; crushed blueberries for blue, etc.

Melt a handful of chocolate chips to use as "paint" to inscribe names and greetings with a clean watercolor brush on birthday cakes, cookies, even sandwiches.

You can also paint melted chocolate on wax paper to be removed when it hardens; and use this technique to make your own chocolate money by painting on clean, greased coins. Apply thickly!

ICE CREAM

I've delayed talking about ice cream as long as I could because I really have mixed emotions about it. Basically my family and I LOVE IT. We love it expensive, cheap, at the local franchise or homemade on the Fourth of July. Our taste buds have a wide range of acceptance . . . gluttony might be a more apt description.

But the facts about ice cream are not all that tasty. More than 1,200 different chemical stabilizers, emulsifiers, neutralizers and artificial colorings and flavorings are legally allowed in commercial ice cream, and ice cream manufacturers are not required by law to list their ingredients. There is no way to know which, if any, of the optional ingredients are in the ice cream you buy. To my mind only those labeled "natural" or "no preservatives or artificial flavorings or colorings added" — usually the more expensive brands — can be identified as natural ice cream. The others tend to be chemical feasts with air whipped into something from the milk family used as a base.

Good ice cream, I discovered when I began to make my own, is fattening because of the large amount of cream, not sugar, that is used. Commercial manufacturers can more readily afford sugar than real cream, and artificial flavorings than fruits.

I have finally opted for the better, more expensive ice creams and I dispense them more frugally. Breyers, a nationally distributed natural brand, rates high in quality. (Incidentally, storing ice cream containers in a plastic bag before putting them in the freezer will help prevent ice crystals from forming.)

Salton manufactures an efficient ice cream maker that works right in the freezer compartment of your refrigerator, thanks to an extension cord you can shut the door on. A major disadvantage of homemade ice cream is that it is apt to freeze too hard. It does not contain chemical emulsifiers to keep it fluffy, and raising your freezer's temperature to soften ice cream would adversely affect other foods in the freezer. However, if you are making your own, here is my favorite base recipe which can be flavored to please your particular taste:

BASIC VANILLA ICE CREAM
2 cups heavy cream
2 eggs, separated
1/2 cup sugar or honey
1 tsp. vanilla
dash of salt

Whip two cups of heavy cream in a blender till fairly thick. Add egg yolks, sweetener, vanilla and salt. Blend to mix. Beat egg whites stiff. Combine with cream mixture. If using a Salton Ice Cream Maker, be sure ingredients are thoroughly chilled before placing in freezing unit. Follow instructions for the ice cream maker.

If you are just using your blender, place blender container holding the mixture into your freezer for 1/2 hour. Take out and blend 1 minute. Repeat this one or two times more, then pour into freezing container. If it doesn't beat efficiently in your blender you will need to use a mixing bowl and an electric beater.

At your grocery store the term "French" ice cream means that a good percentage of egg solids has been added. Ice milk has lower fat content because it contains less milk fat than ice cream. Since less butterfat is often compensated for by more sugar and chemicals, you will not save much in calories.

Sherbet is chemically similar in composition to ice cream but it has a still lower milk content and extra sugar is added to offset a high acid content.

Only water ices contain no milk. Try this easy-to-do recipe:

VERY BERRY ICES
1 pt. fresh berries
3/4 cup sugar or honey
3/4 cup water
1/4 cup orange or lemon juice

Puree fruit in a blender. Heat water and sweetener together to a clear syrup and pour into blender. Mix completely. Freeze in plastic containers or as popsicles.

For other milk-free desserts, see page 110.

ICE CREAM "COOKIE" CONES (A molded cookie that makes a fun holder for a dolop of ice cream)
3 eggs
2 tsp. flavoring (vanilla, almond or maple)
1/4 cup water
3/4 cup brown sugar
3/4 cup whole wheat (or white) flour
2 Tbsp. butter or margarine

Combine above ingredients and mix well with an electric mixer. Before baking make 2-4 conical forms from wadded aluminum foil to use to shape cookies once they are baked. On a greased cookie sheet spread 2 Tbsp. of batter thinly to form a 5-inch in diameter circle. Approximately 4 circles will fit on a cookie sheet. Bake at 300 degrees for 12-15 minutes. Remove cookie sheet from oven and turn "cookies" over and return them to the oven for another 3-5 minutes. Remove from oven and, working quickly, wrap one around the conical mold and pinch bottom. As they cool, they harden. If it becomes hard before you have had a chance to mold them return them to the oven to soften. Store molded cones in an airtight container. This recipe makes 12-18 cones.

DO-IT-YOURSELF SUNDAES
When serving ice cream, offer some of the following toppings:

NUTS. . . . peanuts, walnuts, cashews, etc.

SAUCES . honey, maple syrup, chocolate syrup in small amounts

FRUITS...chopped dates, apricots, berries, banana slices, pineapple, cherries, sliced peaches, etc.

AND OTHER . chocolate chips, granola, shredded coconut,
GOODIES   toasted wheat germ, whipped cream.

I must confess to feeling ambivalent about using dessert as a reward. I understand that this practice may lead to obesity or overeating problems in later life. I do try to prepare foods that will appeal to my children, and I try not to become (too) upset if they don't eat everything. But if, for any reason, they do not finish the better part of their meals, I don't think they should expect to be served dessert. Needless to say, the possibility of "no dessert" is responsible for the consumption of a good deal more fish, soups, salads and vegetables than would otherwise be the case.

I'VE JUST GOT A FEW THINGS FOR YOU TO REMEMBER WHILE I'M OUT....

Sitter Selections . . .
Food That Is

Getting a sitter, getting the kids ready and yourself together—not to mention having dinner done ahead—can make preparing for your evening out an exhausting experience. The following information on what to prepare ahead to feed your kids and the sitter will help with one aspect of getting yourself out of the house on time.

You may catch yourself spitting out a slew of instructions to your sitter as he or she walks in the door. If any instructions are overlooked, it will probably be because a sitter can absorb only so much information per second. If it is important—WRITE IT DOWN.

When your child is small it is important to be specific about what you want your sitter to do. Write it down. Let the sitter know when to expect sleeping, waking, crying and eating. Point out the diapers and your child's favorite diversions. If you expect the baby to be held while being fed from a bottle and burped every three ounces, say so; better yet, write it down. Get the bib out, the food (if appropriate), spoon and any other necessary items so that the sitter will not have to search. If you have an infant, you should have something ready for your sitter to eat that requires little or no preparation, with an alternative that the sitter can make if s/he really doesn't like what you've left.

When your children are older, the sitter will probably eat with them. Such meals should require minimum preparation—you want your sitter to keep an eye on the children, not on the stove (you know the problem you have when you're making dinner!) While your sitters may have more cooking knowledge than you give them credit for, you should keep the menu simple. But don't leave it open-ended. Make specific suggestions if you have not made a meal ahead of time. Tell your sitter where to find the basics s/he may need. Your sitter doesn't know your cupboards like you do.

If you don't want Junior eating sweets or snacks, name your restrictions. You may need to do this for the sitter as well. When the cake you baked for tomorrow's bridge party is off limits, better say so.

The most common sitter fare seems to be peanut butter sandwiches, hot dogs or hamburgers. (And you thought you were the only one!) One way to add variety is with some good freeze-to-please meals, easy to heat or reheat. No doubt you have your favorite casserole dishes, or try these. Actually, why wait for the sitter?

FRENCH TOAST
French toast is a good way to combine eggs, milk and bread. If you use homemade or whole grain bread, you will have to handle it more carefully. These breads are more fragile than white bread after being soaked in the mixture, and break more easily.

Here are two batter recipes:

1 egg		1 egg
1/3 cup milk	**OR**	4 tsp. flour
1/8 tsp. vanilla		1/3 cup milk

The above batters are each enough for approximately 3 slices of bread. For both recipes beat the eggs lightly and add the next two ingredients. Dip bread in mixture and fry in a well greased pan over fairly high heat, browning well on both sides. Or, on a cold morning you can preheat the oven to 500 degrees and bake the dipped bread on a greased pan, turning after the top browns.

For quick freezing, place French toast on a cookie sheet and put in the freezer for a half hour. Remove from the freezer, place in freezer bags and seal well. The advantage of freezing the pieces separately is that they will not stick together in the freezer bag. When ready to use, your babysitter can place the pieces of toast in an oven toaster or regular toaster for a quick main course.

HAMBURGER HEROES

2/3 cup evaporated milk
1 lb. lean ground beef
1/2 cup bread or cracker crumbs, or untoasted wheat germ
1/8 tsp. pepper
1 egg
1/2 cup chopped onion
1 tsp. prepared mustard
1 cup grated cheese
a loaf of French bread

Mix all the filling ingredients together. There will be enough to make 1 large or 2 small hero sandwiches. Cut the French bread loaf in half lengthwise. Spread filling on cut side of each half. Wrap foil around the crusts of the bread-halves, leaving the filling uncovered, and bake on a cookie sheet in a preheated oven at 350 degrees for 25 minutes. Envelop heroes completely in foil when they are to be refrigerated for future use.

Before serving, garnish with cheese strips, mushrooms, olives, peppers, etc. Cut large hero loaves in slices. Smaller loaves may be offered half-a-loaf to a customer.

MEAT LOAF

1-2 lb. hamburger
1 egg, beaten
seasonings (garlic powder, onion soup mix)
1/2 cup untoasted wheat germ
     (or whole wheat bread crumbs or oatmeal)
Optional: 1/4 cup ketchup or spaghetti sauce
                 1/4 cup grated cheese
                 1/2 cup cooked rice
                 1/4-1/2 cup cooked pureed vegetables

(continued on next page)

Mix all ingredients plus any optional ingredients and place in a bread loaf pan. Bake at 350 degrees for 45 minutes. Drain off excess fat. Freeze or refrigerate for reheating if not serving right away.

Variation: Form meatballs from the above ingredients and freeze for future use in meal-size quantities best suited to your family needs.

TUNA BAKED BISCUITS

1 (7 oz.) can of tuna, drained and flaked
1/3 cup mayonnaise
1/4 cup diced celery
1 small carrot, grated
2 Tbsp. sweet relish
1 pkg. (10) refrigerated biscuits

Mix first five ingredients. Separate biscuits. On a lightly floured surface, roll them into the shape of a flat pancake. Spoon tuna salad onto 5 of the circles (or 4, if you prefer a heftier sandwich). Top with remaining circles. Seal by pressing around the edges with fork. Put on an ungreased baking sheet at 375 degrees for 15 minutes or until browned. These can be served warm or cold from the refrigerator. They can also be frozen. To serve, defrost and toast in toaster oven or large oven for a few minutes.

PIZZA

Jazz up a frozen pizza with extra cheese, meat or spices, or make your own pizza.

Pizza crust:

frozen bread dough recipe for a thick pizza crust

Roll or press out one thawed frozen bread dough to fit a round pizza plate or oblong pan. Pinch edges to form a rim. Prick with a fork and brush with oil. Bake at 400 degrees till light brown (about 10 minutes). Freeze crust for future use or add topping and bake at 400 degrees till cheese melts. (Although the frozen French bread dough is good to use, try a darker bread for a nutritious change.)

make your own regular pizza crust

1 1/3 cups warm water
1 pkg. dry yeast
2 Tbsp. salad oil
2 tsp. salt
4 1/3 cups flour (white or half white, half whole wheat)

(continued on next page)

Dissolve yeast in water. Add oil, salt and flour. Knead for 10 minutes. Put dough in a lightly oiled bowl and cover with a damp cloth. Place in a warm place to rise till doubled in size. Punch down. Divide into two balls. Roll or press out into pizza shape. This recipe provides enough dough for two crusts. Bake both pizzas (400 degrees about 10 min.) and freeze one or both, as you choose.

or

Purchase a shelf-stable packaged pizza crust mix at your grocery store.

Pizza Topping

Lightly cover the crust with oil and add a layer of tomato sauce (approximately 1 cup), grated cheese (Mozzarella, Swiss, Monterey Jack or whatever), spices.

Options: cooked sausage, olives, green pepper, mushrooms, onion, crumbled cooked hamburger, sliced tomatoes or any leftovers.

More cheese (such as grated Parmesan) on top. Bake at 400 degrees for 10-20 minutes till cheese melts.

FRIED CHICKEN

There's always chicken . . . yours, the Colonel's or the grocery's frozen fried variety. (Nutritionally speaking, boiled is better, but you might lose your baby sitter.)

CHEESE/BACON SANDWICH

1 (8 oz.) can refrigerated crescent rolls
3/4 cup (3 oz.) shredded Swiss cheese
3/4 cup shredded Mozzarella or Montery Jack cheese
1 egg, beaten
1 Tbsp. minced or chopped onion
3/4 cup milk
1 4-oz. can (1/2 cup) mushroom stems and pieces, drained (optional)
6 slices bacon, drained and crumbled
1 Tbsp. chives/parsley

Preheat oven to 375 degrees. Separate crescent dough into two rectangles. Place in ungreased 13 x 9-inch pan. Press over bottom and 1/2 inch up sides to form crust, sealing perforations.

(continued on next page)

Sprinkle cheeses over dough. Combine egg, onion, milk, and mushrooms and pour over cheese. Sprinkle with bacon and chives or parsley. Bake 22-28 minutes until crust is deep golden brown and filling is set. Cool 5 minutes before cutting into squares. Makes 4-6 servings. Refrigerate leftovers.

Hint: To make ahead, prepare, cover and refrigerate up to two hours, then bake as directed. To reheat, cover loosely with foil and pop jnto 375 degree oven for 20-25 minutes.

For a cold meal-in-one dish:

MACARONI SALAD
        1 cup elbow macaroni
        4 cups water
        1/2 cucumber, diced
        2 sliced hard-cooked eggs
        1/2 cup diced cheese
        1/2 cup diced celery
        1/2 cup grated carrots
        1/2 cup mayonnaise
        1 tsp. lemon juice

Cook macaroni in 4 cups of boiling water according to directions on package. Drain and chill. Stir in other ingredients including mayonnaise and lemon juice combined. This will serve 2 hungry children and one babysitter well.

HOMEMADE TV DINNERS

Recycle your TV dinner trays*—the aluminum ones with divided compartments.
Fill with:

Main Course (precooked)	Vegetables	Other
hot dog	peas	garlic bread
hamburger	carrots	roll
macaroni and cheese	corn	cooked rice
your child's favorite	squash	cooked noodles
hot dish	mashed potatoes	

Cook fresh vegetables or repack the trays from bags of the frozen variety.

Let the babysitter pull out the appropriate number of trays before mealtime to heat in the oven for 20-40 minutes at 350 degrees.

*Yes, I admit to buying TV dinners occasionally.

PASTIES (not "pasteries") A meal-all-in one! A portable pot pie!

Pasty dough

2 cups flour
2 tsp. baking powder
1 tsp. salt
2/3 cup shortening
1 Tbsp. lemon juice
1 egg yolk unbeaten
1/2 cup hot water

Combine flour, baking powder and salt. Cut shortening into mixture. Add lemon juice, egg yolk and hot water and mix well. Divide dough into 4-5 round balls. (HINT: Defrosted frozen bread dough works well here.)

Pasty filling

1 lb. round steak, diced
1/2 lb. pork steak, diced
1 large onion, chopped
5-6 med.-sized potatoes, diced
4-5 diced carrots
seasonings

On a floured surface, roll a ball of the pasty dough into a circle. Place a handful of filling onto one-half of the circle. Top with a dot of butter. Fold dough over (as for a turnover) and crimp edges. Prick top of crust. Bake at 400 degrees for 20 minutes, then @ 350 degrees for 40 minutes until juice dries up around pasty.

For freezing, bake a little less. Wrap in foil. Leave in foil to reheat and cook until heated through.

Hint: This is not a quickie recipe. You can split up the preparation time by dicing the filling ingredients prior to making the pasties (such as the day before). Either way, they are well worth the effort!

Using paper plates when sitters are over may well make everyone happier. If you expect dishes rinsed or put in the dishwasher or put away, you will have to specify. Sitters don't enjoy doing dishes any more than you do!

Eating
En Route

Summer vacation! Visit to grandma! The long planned cross-country trip! Whether traveling by car, bus or plane, eating will be a major activity (or trauma) on any trip. No matter what games or activities you plan, food will be the star attraction. Be prepared! Food requests often come within 15 minutes of being en route, closely following the question, "Are we there yet?"

Save time by referring to the following list before you begin your trip. Despite the convenience of convenience foods while traveling, good-for-you foods are as easy to carry and more enjoyable to eat.

PROTEINS

Hard-cooked eggs
Cheeses—including the triangular wrapped Gruyere sections, and fresh curds, etc.
Nuts
Peanut butter balls (see page 17)
A jar of peanut butter
Beef jerky
A roll of salami (not advisable on bus or airplane if you wish to remain in the good graces of your fellow travelers)
Cooked cold chicken

Note: Avoid sandwich spreads made with mayonnaise if you are not carrying a cooler. Unrefrigerated, they spoil quickly.

FRUITS AND VEGETABLES

Apples (cored to save waste and mess. Good stuffed with
    peanut butter or soft cheese)
Pears (can be cored also)
Seedless grapes
Raisins
Fruit leather, homemade (see page 44) or commercial
Dried apple rings (see page 43)
Bananas (never pack at the bottom of your bag!)
Navel oranges (pre-cut)
Carrot and celery sticks (immersed in cold water for a long
    trip; otherwise just washed and packed in a plastic bag)

ETC . . . ETC . . . ETC

Finger Jello (see page 42. Can go unrefrigerated four hours)
Soft pretzels (see page 45. Less crumbly than the other kind)
Packaged granola bars
Popcorn (in small individual bags)
Gorp . . . a mixture of nuts, raisins and chocolate chips
Pepperidge Farm Fish Crackers
Small boxes of dry cereal (see page 122 for those with lower
    sugar content)

Crackers are usually crumbly, especially saltines. Nevertheless,
a fun and easy snack for traveling is a box of crackers (try Wheat
Thins or Triscuits) and a bottle of squirt cheese. Squirt cheese,
while not recommended as standard fare (more air and water
than cheese), can be very appropriate for traveling. Mom or dad
can dispense the cheese on the crackers in designs, letters or numbers.

Bagels are the least crumbly travelers, ideal for sandwiches
when sliced and filled with cream cheese, sliced cheese, peanut
butter, etc.

DRINKS

One wise mother I know of carried only water—ice cold water—
when traveling. Spilled, it wasn't sticky. Nor did it stain. Since
water appealed less than sweetened drinks, it was requested less
frequently and subsequent "potty stops" were fewer.

Other drink ideas:

Small individual cans of juice can be frozen beforehand and allowed to thaw along the way. Drink them cold but not frozen.

Those lovely Airpots travel well and make accidents more easily avoidable when dispensing drinks. (They must travel in an upright position.)

Tupperware plastic glasses with spill-proof lids are terrific travelers for drink or food. Or just fill them with ice cubes to melt enroute for cold water.

A camper canteen can be an exciting and personal drinking container.

Fill a plastic juice-type container half-way with water and then freeze it. Remove from freezer and fill it to the top with water. The water will stay cold all day as the block of ice melts very slowly.

Recycle your plastic lemon or lime juice containers. Empty the juice concentrate, remove the insert (try an ice pick), rinse and fill with water or juice. Replace insert. Children can squirt the liquid into their mouths with a minimum of drip. Put cap on to close and prevent leaking.

Artificially sweetened soda in cans. The clear pop doesn't stain when spilled.

FORGET MILK! It is not easy on the tummy when traveling.

MEAL IDEAS

One of the nicest ways to eat enroute is to picnic. Food for easy-to-make roadside picnics can either be brought or purchased in grocery stores along the way. At a picnic the service is always speedy. No tipping is required. Children are free to roam and to get needed exercise. Maybe you can even find a park with a playground.

Car meals are best controlled by keeping the food container next to the non-driving parent. Food dispensed one course at a time helps pass the hours and keeps down the mess.

An empty shoe box makes a good lap tray.

Sandwiches are easier for children to handle when made on cocktail-sized breads.

If you need a quick breakfast to get you on the road early, bring along granola mixed with powdered milk (approximately 2 Tbsp. powdered milk to one cup granola). Obviously, this works with other dry cereals as well. Serve in paper cups or paper bowls. Add water and you have an INSTANT BREAKFAST. Don't forget the spoons.

FAST-FOOD RESTAURANTS

For most people, eating enroute means stopping at fast-food restaurants. Their speed is a blessing to parents of hungry children with short attention spans, but nutritional balance is wanton. These restaurants supply ample protein accompanied by excess calories from frying (French fries) and sugars (sodas and shakes). Missing are the nutrients of fruits and vegetables. This is the best argument for buying burgers with lettuce, tomato and onion.

The typical fast-food meal is not devoid of food value; rather, it is somewhat unbalanced. One hundred percent of your FDA carbohydrate (sugar and starch) daily need will be met, but little of your vitamin C need, for instance. Dependence on such restaurants for your primary nourishment is unhealthy.

Most of us can get nearly half our day's calorie requirement from one meal at a fast-food restaurant. And when traveling by car there is no opportunity to work it off. High fat, low fiber meals accompanied by little exercise are just not healthful. So supplement! Don't hesitate to bring some fruits or vegetables from your car or your home. Apples, for one, fit easily into pockets. Avoid French fries as a side dish. Also, patronize those restaurants that provide salad bars. Buy milk (or tea for mom and dad) for a better balanced meal instead of colas or chocolate shakes. Or buy juice or low-cal sodas. Look for water fountains and ask for glasses of water.

Consumers Report in May 1975, printed a nutritional evaluation of fast-food chains. Top of the "most for your money" list was a pizza franchise. Their menu offered the most protein in each average meal with the least excess fats. The calories weren't excessively high. It was not perfect (no vitamin C) and, unfortunately, salt use was highest of all the restaurants visited.

Other findings:

Diners who are on low sodium diets or wish to avoid salt would do well to shun these restaurants since all dishes are salted. In fact, a typical meal may contain as much as 1-1/2 tsp. of table salt.

Fried chicken meals contained more protein than hamburger meals, but deep frying produced the highest fat content.

The least protein (albeit sufficient for one meal's requirements) came from fried fish fillets. The fried fish meal, however, was lowest in calories.

The ratings of hamburger chains were fairly similar . . . high in calories, low in vitamins and minerals usually supplied by fruits and vegetables.

Fast-food chains are growing in popularity as evidenced by their appearance at every available corner. They can be part of eating enroute, but not the major part if we wish to have a balanced diet. If you wish to maintain a clean car (good luck!), avoid eating at drive-in restaurants. Also you don't get the chance to stretch!

If sit-down restaurants are part of your travel plans, you may want to make some pre-trip eat-out practice jaunts. Remembering to avoid arrival at traditional meal hours may save long waits and jumpy children. The same children who crave food constantly while traveling in a car may not finish their plate in a restaurant.

Don't rule out hotel room service. Occasionally, despite expense, the advantages and convenience may be well worthwhile.

WAIT! One last thing before you go. Consider these other bringalongs:

Plastic bags . . . for garbage, motion sickness, dirty laundry; for storing foods, toys, wet bathing suits, souvenirs, etc.
Disposable moist towelettes . . . for clean-up (a damp wash cloth in a plastic bag serves the same purpose).
Sugar-free gum . . . or one small package of hard candies to settle a stomach, keep ears from popping in an airplane, as a hold-over in a slow serving restaurant.
Jump rope . . . for quick, concentrated exercise during breaks on car trips.

Metal cake pan with sliding cover . . . unexcelled container for pencils, paper, crayons, scissors, glue stick, and the top doubles as a writing surface. Will also hold activity books and reading material. (Reading in cars causes some children to become nauseated.)

A magic slate.

Dot to Dot games . . . in books, on graph paper, or do-it-yourself.

Repacking game in a bag or smaller container will conserve on car space.

Playdough . . . in small amounts. Travels well in small plastic bag.

Binoculars or telescopes . . . The toy kinds are o.k. but real ones are more fun.

A flashlight . . . can be a fun toy as well as a bedtime security in a strange room.

Pipe cleaners . . . for sculpturing.

Card games.

A tape recorder . . . to verbalize and record impressions of significant places or happenings.

AND WHAT EVER ELSE WORKS FOR YOU!

Cooking
For Kids
In A Microwave

If you have used a microwave oven you have learned what a terrific helper it is for a parent. Microwaves are safe (due to government regulations and fail-safe doors on ovens) convenient, fast and are becoming more easily affordable. The questions are whether you have room in your kitchen and room in your budget. Standard ovens are being made with microwave units built in. A microwave is definitely a boon. It is one of the few true labor-saving devices on the market. Foods tend to cook quicker, re-heat instantly and defrost when you've only begun to contemplate dinner at four in the afternoon. A microwave also saves the work of cleaning dishes that you would otherwise have to use because many foods can be prepared in their serving dishes.

When you need to feed a family of six or more a microwave may not help your meal preparation as much as it will for a smaller family. The more you put into the microwave the longer it takes to cook.

A microwave can help you as a parent right from the beginning.

FOR BABY

Heating the bottle:
- one 8-ounce bottle at room temperature, 15-30 seconds.
- one 8-ounce bottle cold from the refrigerator, 30-60 seconds. (Remove nipple and screw cap before heating.)

    P.S. Remember, however, that a cold bottle doesn't usually matter to the baby, only to the mother. (Just don't get it too hot!)

Heating baby food:
- Homemade frozen cubes or plops of pureed baby food can be warmed in approximately 60-90 seconds.
- A jar of baby food with cap removed can be warmed in approximately 30 seconds; a little longer when taken cold from the refrigerator. Three jars in a circle will heat in 90 seconds. When buying commercial baby food, try to select from the basic fruits, vegetables and strained meats, avoiding combination meals and desserts.

BREAKFAST

GRANOLA
Toasting granola in the microwave is fast and efficient. Because of the way it is uniformly heated, when it has cooled you will find you have granola that is crunchy and lumpy instead of flaky.

   3 cups uncooked oatmeal
   1 cup untoasted wheat germ
   1 cup unsweetened coconut
   2 Tbsp. cinnamon
   2 Tbsp. brown sugar
   1/4 cup powdered milk
   1/3 cup honey
   1/3 cup oil
   1 tsp. vanilla

Mix all of the dry ingredients together in a large, shallow glass dish. Combine the honey, oil and vanilla and heat in the microwave for 30 seconds. Drizzle this warm liquid over the dry ingredients, coating thoroughly, using your hands to stir. Place this mixture in your microwave for approximately 10-15 minutes. Cool completely before removing from dish and store in an airtight container. (In a standard oven, toast at 250 degrees for one hour or 300 degrees for a half hour, stirring several times during the toasting process.)

   Variation: Seeds, nuts, raisins or dates, when desired, should be added after the mixture has cooled.

PANCAKES AND WAFFLES
A stack of pancakes made ahead can be reheated in a matter of seconds. Waffles reheat even more quickly.

OATMEAL

>3/4 cup water
>5 Tbsp. oatmeal (not the "Quick" kind)
>1 Tbsp. butter
>1 tsp. brown sugar
>milk

Stir water and oatmeal together in a serving bowl. Microwave 1 1/2 minutes. Stir, add butter, microwave until butter is melted. Remove from oven, add the sugar and as much milk as needed.

OR

Make a large quantity of creamy old-fashioned oatmeal the night before, refrigerate, then reheat in individual serving dishes for breakfast the next day.

MUENSTER SOUP

Microwave a hunk of favorite cheese (my kids prefer Muenster but any will work) in a cereal bowl till just melted. Serve with a spoon, and either crackers or toast!

BACON

Bacon is a fatty, though delicious, food that can be cooked so easily in a microwave. Put two or three layers of paper toweling on the bottom of a glass serving dish. Lay your bacon on this, then cover with two more layers of paper toweling. Microwave for 1-2 minutes for 4-6 slices. Timing depends on the quantity of bacon you are cooking and your personal taste. The bacon browns nicely, the grease is absorbed by the toweling, and you have not splattered your stovetop.

LUNCH

HOT DOGS ON A STICK

Insert a popsicle stick in the end of a hot dog and cook on a paper plate.

>1 frankfurter, a little over half-a-minute
>2 frankfurters, 60-90 seconds
>5 frankfurters, 2-3 minutes

(continued on next page)

HAMBURGERS

Shape one pound of ground beef into four patties. Coat with soy sauce or basting sauce to "brown" burger. Place on a 9-inch glass pie plate or square baking dish. Cover with waxed paper, paper plate or paper towel and cook approximately 3 minutes. Turn hamburgers and rotate the dish. Cook 3 minutes longer until the patties are done. Hamburgers should not be overdone. Like most meats, they continue to cook after removal from the oven.

HOT SWISS TUNA ON BUNS

    1 can tuna, drained
    1/2 cup shredded Swiss or Cheddar cheese
    1/4 cup mayonnaise
    1 tsp. lemon juice
    4 hamburger buns
    Optional: Chopped olives or sweet relish

Combine tuna, mayonnaise, lemon juice and shredded cheese. Divide mixture among the four buns and place them in the microwave on a paper towel, leaving space between the buns. Microwave for 60-90 seconds. Cheese heats quickly in a microwave. Seconds make a difference. You know it is overcooked when it is rubbery.

MELTED CHEESE SANDWICH

    2 slices whole wheat bread, preferably frozen slices of
        cheese (Muenster, Cheddar, Swiss, etc.)

Place cheese slices between bread slices. Put on a paper plate and microwave 30 seconds or until cheese starts to melt. Let cool, cut in halves or quarters, and serve.

Variation: Use corn (not flour) tortillas instead of bread.

DINNER

BAKED POTATOES

Baking potatoes in almost no time at all is one of the microwave oven's best accomplishments. When you find it easier to bake potatoes than to heat the frozen French fries, you will surely serve this tasty vegetable—rich in vitamin C, iron and many other vitamins and minerals—in its more wholesome form oftener than its fattier, more processed "relative."

To cook: Use medium-sized potatoes, scrub them well and prick several times with a fork. Arrange on a paper towel or paper plate. If you have several potatoes, arrange them in a circle with at least one inch of space between each, and bake as follows:

1 potato, 3-4 minutes
2 potatoes, 5-6 minutes
3 potatoes, 8-9 minutes
4 potatoes, 10-11 minutes
5 potatoes, 13-15 minutes

The larger the potato the longer it will take to cook. Potatoes continue to cook after they are removed from the oven and they keep hot for quite a long time.

CORN-ON-THE-COB

When cooking corn in the microwave you can either remove the outer husks and silk and wrap each individual corn ear in a paper towel or you can simply open the fresh corn, remove the silk and rewrap it in the outer husks. One ear of corn takes approximately 2 minutes and two ears, 4 minutes.

LAZYBONES APPLESAUCE

4 cooking apples
2 Tbsp. sweetener
Optional: cinnamon to taste

Place 4 clean, cored, apples on a glass baking dish. Microwave 6-8 minutes until apples are soft. Let cool. Peel off skin or scrape soft insides from apple skin into glass dish. Mash with a fork. Add sweetener, if needed, and cinnamon, if desired.

VEGETABLES

Vegetables cooked by microwave need little or no water, which makes the oven the most exciting vegetable cooker to arrive on the market so far. All the nutrition stays in the vegetables until you eat them. When cooking vegetables, a general time rule would be 6-8 minutes (stirring once or twice) for four servings in a covered dish. However, some vegetables—frozen peas, for instance—can be microwaved in individual small cups in 30-60 seconds.

CANNED SOUPS

Dilute canned soup with an equal quantity of water or milk. In a single bowl or cup, heat in the microwave for two minutes.

HINT: To heated soups add grated cheese, croutons, popcorn, tortilla chips or oyster crackers.

DESSERTS

Desserts are not one of the stronger areas where a microwave is useful. (Maybe this fact makes it the perfect oven!) Cakes cook lumpishly, can scorch and require repeated turning during the baking period. There are a couple of desserts, though, that you may want to try.

BAKED APPLE
    1 apple
    1 Tbsp. butter
    1/4 tsp. cinnamon
    1/2 tsp. brown sugar

Core and peel skin from the top of each apple. A single apple can be baked in a ceramic or glass dish. Fill the center of each apple with butter, sugar and cinnamon. Cook, uncovered, in the microwave 3-4 minutes for one apple, 5-7 minutes for two, 8-10 for four. Before serving you may wish to top them with a little milk, cream or ice cream.

PINEAPPLE UPSIDE-DOWN CAKE
    2 Tbsp. butter or margarine
    1/4 cup packed brown sugar
    1 (8 oz.) can sliced pineapple, drained, which has been packed in its own juice (or well-drained crushed pineapple)
    Optional: 1/2 cup walnut halves
    1 1/3 cup flour
    1 cup sugar
    2 tsp. baking powder
    1/3 cup powdered milk
    1/2 cup cooking oil
    1 egg
    1 tsp. vanilla
    1/2 cup of drained pineapple juice

Melt butter and brown sugar in an 8-inch round or square glass pan. Microwave 1 minute. Smooth mixture evenly over bottom of pan. Add drained pineapple (reserve the liquid) and nuts, if using. Combine balance of ingredients. Pour batter over pineapple mixture and spread evenly and gently. Microwave 8 to 10 minutes, turning pan often. If the center still looks moist, microwave another 2 minutes. Remove from the oven and let cool 1 minute before turning out on a platter. Serve hot or cool, with or without a creamy topping.

PEACHY DELIGHT
    1 peach half
    1/4 tsp. butter
    1 tsp. brown sugar
Put butter and brown sugar inside the peach half and microwave 1 minute for one, 2 minutes for two, and 3 minutes for four peach halves.

CARMEL BANANAS
Warm a tablespoon of butter and a tablespoon of maple syrup together in a dish for 20-30 seconds. Coat a peeled banana in this mixture and then heat it for one minute in the microwave. Serve with a dash of lemon juice.

SNACKS

UNPIZZA SNACK
In a mug place a spoonful of spaghetti sauce and a handful of grated Mozzarella cheese, heat 60 seconds and eat with a spoon.

WISE CRAX
Melt cheese on a graham cracker.

CHEESIE CHIPPIES
Toss taco chips with a cup or two of grated American cheese and microwave until the cheese melts.

Talking about cheese—a slice of American, or any variety, placed on a Sloppy Joe, tuna sandwich, egg salad, etc., and microwaved 30 seconds will help prevent the filling from spilling.

DRINKS

No longer must you wait forever for the frozen orange juice you forgot to take out the night before to defrost in time for breakfast. After removing the top, place the can in the microwave oven for 30-60 seconds. (This is assuming that the whole can is not made out of metal.) Mix with water as directed on the can and serve at once.

HOT CHOCOLATE

Fill a plastic or ceramic cup three-quarters full with milk. Add 1-2 tablespoons cocoa mix or carob drink mix. Marshmallows are optional (mighty optional!). Microwave 1-2 minutes and stir when removed from oven. The neat thing is that you can make hot chocolate with milk because it will not scorch. No need to use the envelope mixes that contain dry milk as well as many other ingredients which are not necessary.

HOT APPLE JUICE WITH CINNAMON

Fill glass, ceramic or plastic mug with apple juice, insert a cinnamon stick or dash of cinnamon and heat in the microwave for 1 minute.

LET THE KIDS DO THE COOKING

The microwave is a terrific oven for young children to use. As soon as they are old enough to understand directions (around 5 or 6 years of age) they can help prepare many foods themselves. They can try recipes such as hot dogs, grilled cheese sandwiches or making their own hot drink. Children will not burn themselves on the oven because a microwave never gets hot. Nor does the dish; only the food.

Browning plates are becoming more popular with the use of microwaves. They brown the food they cook by becoming super hot themselves. A browning plate might be dangerous for a young child to use as s/he could be burned.

Among other uses the microwave has in your kitchen:

PICNICS

Microwave hot dogs, hamburgers, corn-on-the-cob, etc., wrap in aluminum foil and pack in your picnic basket. The food will stay hot quite a while.

FAST FOOD RESTAURANTS

If your spouse has just brought dinner home from a fast food restaurant, the whole bag (cold drinks removed, of course) can be inserted in the microwave oven, (assuming none of the foods are wrapped in aluminum foil) and reheated in a few minutes. Or, if you prefer, simply put individual servings on plates and microwave each plate, one at a time, approximately 30-60 seconds.

When using the microwave oven it is better to set the time on the low side a second or two than to risk overcooking your food.

FRINGE BENEFITS
To soften butter:
> Place stick of butter or margarine in a glass measuring cup or non-metallic mixing bowl. Heat 10 seconds, let stand 10 seconds. Repeat till shortening reaches required softness.

To soften raisins:
> Pour a little water over 2 cups raisins. Heat uncovered 2 minutes, let stand 2 minutes. Drain and use.

To roast raw peanuts:
> Place 3 cups of raw peanuts which have been tossed with 1 Tbsp. oil in a shallow baking dish. Microwave for 15 to 20 minutes, stirring nuts every 2 minutes. You must let them cool before tasting as they will still seem "raw" when warm.

To roast chestnuts:
> Make an X slash in each of 18-24 chestnuts. Place them in a single layer on an appropriate dish. Microwave (uncovered) for 1 minute. Turn the nuts and microwave another minute. Stir nuts one last time and microwave for another minute. If done, they will be soft when squeezed. Let them cool 5 minutes before peeling to eat.

To empty containers:
> To really empty many containers (honey, ketchup, etc.) heat until more "liquidy" and pour out.

To clarify honey:
> Clarify honey turned to sugar by heating jar without cap for 1 minute.

To warm foods:
> Foods can be warmed in (and the warmth retained) in a small wide-mouth **all plastic** thermo container.

To soften brown sugar:
> Place bag of sugar in microwave for 30-60 seconds.

> HINT: For mom, save leftover tea or coffee in glass jars. Refrigerate, then reheat as needed.

If Your Child Can't Drink Milk

It's surprising how little practical information is available to parents of children who can't drink milk. Milk intolerance is a common problem that defies the slogan "MILK IS FOR EVERYBODY". It is not. Actually, the majority of the world's population cannot tolerate cows milk. Most able are those of Western European descent and even among this group a significant percentage (20%) can't tolerate milk. Symptoms such as abdominal pain, bloating, gas, diarrhea, or nausea may well be related to the ingestion of cow's milk. This intolerance is due to an inability to digest the natural sugar in milk and is referred to as "lactose intolerance". An enzyme in the intestinal lining named "lactase", breaks down lactose (milk sugar) into simple digestible sugars. When lactase is completely absent (a rare condition) or present in low concentrations (more common), consumption of milk products may cause discomfort. In a young child, an intestinal infection can cause a temporary reduction of lactase. (This is one reason why doctors eliminate milk when a child has diarrhea).

The amount of milk tolerable to those with lactose intolerance varies with the level of lactase in the intestine. For example, some persons who cannot digest moderate amounts of milk can tolerate natural yogurt or aged cheeses.

It is generally believed that mother's milk never causes diges-
tive problems for a new baby. However, if a baby has a complete lactase deficiency (which is very rare), s/he will not be able
to tolerate even breast milk. Fortunately today, soy-based formulas are available for babies having trouble digesting milk for
whatever reason. Infant soy formula is balanced to provide
good growth. Feeding soy formula to an infant is an uncompli-
cated task because, like other ready-to-feed formulas, it is available in liquid form. Soy formula or soy milk powder is made from
soy beans, a good source of protein and calcium which is easy
to digest.

When solid foods replace formula and food choices broaden,
selection becomes challenging. If all milk is restricted, it will be
necessary to read labels on every package of processed food
before buying. **Here is a list of foods which contain milk or
milk-sugar by-products.** Some are obvious inclusions, others
are surprising.

> Milk (cream, sour cream, cream cheeses, skim, evapor-
> ated, condensed, butter, cheese, buttermilk, pow-
> dered, yogurt, most margarines)
> Imitation sour cream
> Ice cream, ice milk, sherbet
> Cream soups and chowders
> Gravies
> Frostings
> Buttered syrups
> Milk chocolate
> Candy containing milk or milk chocolate
> Caramels, toffees
> Some chewing gums
> Cookies, boxed and bakery
> Most breads (important to check labels)
> Many crackers
> Popovers
> Croutons
> Prepared mixes for baked goods
> Canned spaghetti and other pastas
> Most hot dogs, bolognas, liverwurst and other cold cuts
> Canned meats, spreads
> Foods fried in batter
> Frozen fish sticks
> Pressed chicken rolls

Vegetables frozen in butter or cheese sauces
Frozen egg substitutes
Many dry cereals
Salad dressing when cheese has been added
Many sugar substitutes (Sweet and Low)
Molasses

The words on labels to watch for are: milk, lactose, non-fat dry milk solids, curds, whey, margarine, butter, calcium caseinate.

Again, keep in mind that milk intolerance is often a matter of degree. Some children tolerate more milk products than others. Fortunately some children outgrow this but for others it is a question of adjusting milk and milk-product intake to a comfortable level. A complete lactose intolerance present at birth will not be outgrown, however.

It is essential to consult with a pediatrician before removing milk from a child's diet. Do not make a diagnosis yourself!

Discuss your child's diet with your pediatrician to be sure that enough protein and calcium, the main nutritional benefits of milk, are being provided from your limited food selection. Other protein rich foods are meat, poultry, eggs, dried beans, nuts, peanut butter, fish, pork and lamb. Milk and milk-products are our most important source of calcium. Although minimal compared with milk, other calcium rich foods are sardines, soybeans, dried figs, cauliflower, broccoli, green olives, spinach, dates, dried apricots, raisins, dried prunes, limes, scallions, and green beans.

In order to get roughly the equivalent of calcium contained in 1 quart of milk, one would have to eat any of the following foods:
      3 loaves of bread
      2 lbs. of dried figs
      4 lbs. of broccoli
      4 lbs. of dates
      9-10 lbs. of green beans

If your child's diet is completely milk-free your pediatrician, no doubt, will add a calcium supplement. Calcium supports bone growth which is crucial during fast growth years.

There is one product available which does make milk digestible for the lactose-intolerant person. It is called LACT-AID
and comes as a small packet of lactase enzyme which can be
added to a quart of milk. It will break down 75 percent of the
lactose present. In some parts of the country fresh milk treated
with Lact-Aid may be available in grocery stores. For two sam-
ples of Lact-Aid and literature on it, send 25 cents to SugarLo
Company, 3540 Atlantic Avenue, P.O. Box 1017, Atlantic City,
NJ 08404.

Another newly developed product is called Milk Digestant. It
is a tablet of lactase plus rennin that has to be taken before or
during a meal (afterwards is too late) to aid in the digestion of
milk and milk products. It is only available through health food
stores which must get it from Malabar-Cor-ron Products, 16321
Pacific Coast Highway No. 147, Pacific Palisades, CA 90272.

A lactose intolerance is only one of several reasons your child
might be taken off of milk. Some children are simply "allergic"
(sneeze, wheez, etc.) to milk. Regardless of the origins of your
problem, here are some cooking ideas to make life a bit more
tolerable.

COOKING MILK-FREE

In cooking you can very often substitute another liquid for
the quantity of milk called for. Soy powdered milk can be
reconstituted and is available in health food stores, supermarkets or drug stores. Some non-dairy coffee lighteners are useful
but be sure the one you select omits lactose. Infant soy formula
may be palatable in some recipes or used on cereals.* When a
recipe calls for milk or cream, try water, chicken stock, beef
stock, wine or fruit juices. Orange juice and apple juice work
nicely in many recipes for baked products. With a bit of experimenting you'll find substitutes of your own that work.

*Ross Laboratories (625 Cleveland Ave.; Columbus, Ohio 43216) has available a book-
let called "Good Eating for the Milk-Sensitive Person", offering recipes using their soy
infant formula.

BREAKFAST

Use margarines that don't contain milk or milk products, such as Mazola salt-free margarine found in your grocery's refrigerated dairy case or freezer section.

FRENCH TOAST
   1 egg
   1/2 tsp. water or orange juice
   a dash of cinnamon
   a drop of vanilla
   1 slice of milk-free bread
   1 Tbsp. milk-free margarine
Beat egg in a shallow bowl with water or juice, cinnamon and vanilla. Soak bread in liquid till all is absorbed. Melt milk-free margarine or shortening in a pan. Brown soaked toast on one side, flip and brown on the other. Serve with syrup (no butter) or jam, or make a sandwich by using a slice of ham or bacon between slices of French toast.

PANCAKES
   Make your own batter. Most prepared mixes contain dry milk solids. Instead of milk, substitute coffee lightener, soy milk, or orange juice mixed with water. Add corn oil, vegetable shortening or milk-free margarine. You'll hardly notice the difference from pancakes made with milk.

BANANA BREAD
   3/4 cup vegetable shortening
   1/2 cup brown sugar
   1/2 cup white sugar
   2 eggs
   1/2 tsp. vanilla or orange extract
   1 cup very ripe bananas, mashed
   1 cup whole wheat flour
   3/4 cup white flour
   a dash of salt
Cream shortening and sugar. Beat in eggs and extract. Add mashed bananas. Sift in flour, baking powder and salt. Mix thoroughly. Bake in a greased loaf pan at 350 degrees for 55 minutes.

MUFFINS
Follow your usual recipe or any given on boxes of milk-free cereal but use the liquid of your choice instead of milk.

Of course there are always hot cereals (not instant Cream of Wheat; read labels carefully) and soft or hard-cooked eggs. You also need to read dry cereal labels carefully because so many, including most granola types, contain milk. Milk substitutes, even orange juice, taste pretty good over dry cereal. Keep in mind that most egg substitutes contain milk.

LUNCHES

Peanut butter is a good protein source, fine on milk-free bread or toast. Also meats, egg salad, soups (not cream ones), milk-free hot dogs (the kosher kind), milk-free cold cuts, mild chili con carne, spaghetti with meat sauce (use any leftover meat), tacos (the shells should be milk-free) with meat, shredded lettuce or spinach.

TUNABURGERS
     1 can tuna, drained
     1 egg
     1/2 tsp. lemon juice
     1/3 cup wheat germ
     a pinch of paprika
Mix ingredients, adding a small amount of liquid if necessary to hold mixture together. Form into patties and pan fry in milk-free shortening.

TUNA MOUSSE
     1/4 cup cool water
     2 tsp. gelatin, unflavored
     1 cup hot water
     1 Tbsp. chopped onion (optional)
     1 tsp. lemon juice
     1/2 tsp. dill weed
     paprika (optional but helps color and flavor)
     1 (6 1/2 oz.) can tuna, drained
     1/3 cup mayonnaise

(continued on next page)

In 1/4 cup cool water, in a one-cup measure, sprinkle gelatin to soften (5 minutes). Then add very hot water to one-cup line and stir to dissolve gelatin. Pour gelatin, onion, lemon juice, dill and paprika in container of electric blender. Blend at high speed for 15 seconds. Turn off. Add flaked tuna and mayonnaise. Blend on high for 30 seconds, adding 1/3 cup more water if necessary to blend. Makes 2 cups of mixture which you can mold and chill in a small bowl or fancy shape mold till set. Serve on bread, crackers or plain lettuce and tomato. Tuna mousse goes down easily when throats are sore or children are teething and can't chew.

TUNA CASSEROLE (Make your own white sauce — no cream soups!)

1 Tbsp. milk-free margarine
1 Tbsp. flour
1 can clam broth or chicken broth or either mixed with water

3 oz. noodles, cooked
1 can tuna fish
peas (optional), cooked, canned or frozen
paprika and/or bread crumbs
season with celery salt or garlic powder or onion flakes

For white sauce, melt margarine in saucepan over moderate heat. Add flour, stirring and blending till smooth and slightly browned. Slowly add either 1 cup clam broth OR 1 cup chicken broth. Cook till thickened. Combine with rest of ingredients, pour into 1 1/2 quart casserole dish, top with milk-free bread crumbs and paprika. Bake at 325 degrees for 40 minutes.

BREAD CRUMBS

Instead of using a batter containing milk, try dipping fish, meat, or whatever, first in seasoned flour, then in egg beaten with a slight amount of water, then into your homemade milk-free bread crumbs. This can be done ahead and refrigerated till cooking time.

YOGURT CHEESE
1 (8 oz.) container of plain yogurt.
cheese cloth

In the evening, after the dinner dishes are done, spread out a 12 inch square double thickness of cheese cloth and place contents of yogurt container in the center. Bring four corners together, close and hang from the sink's water faucet overnight. In the morning remove the "cheese" from the cloth and refrigerate until ready to use. If yogurt is a food your child can tolerate, this recipe becomes a sort of cream cheese base for many spreads and dips.

DESSERTS

MILK FREE CAKE (also known as the Puddle Cake)
1 1/2 cups flour (white or half white, half whole wheat)
1 cup sugar
1 tsp. baking soda
3 Tbsp. cocoa or carob powder
1 tsp. vanilla
1 tsp. vinegar
6 Tbsp. cooking oil
1 cup water

Sift flour, sugar, soda and cocoa into an ungreased 8 x 10 inch cake pan. With a mixing spoon, make three holes in the dry mixture. Place vanilla in the first hole, vinegar in the second and oil in the third. Pour water over all and stir with a fork to moisten dry ingredients. Do not beat. Bake at 350 degrees for 35 minutes.

"MARGARINE-CREAM" FROSTING
1/2 cup (1 stick) milk-free margarine
2 cups powdered sugar
1 egg yolk, well beaten
a drop of vanilla and/or 1/3 cup cocoa powder (not drink mix)

Cream margarine and sugar till very fluffy. Add egg yolk and beat. Then beat in vanilla and chocolate. For decorative frosting you can use vegetable shortening which will yield white instead of off-white frosting.

UNRESTRICTED PEANUT BUTTER COOKIES
2 egg whites, slightly beaten
1 cup sugar
1 1/2 cups peanut butter
Optional: 1/2 cup toasted wheat germ

Combine above ingredients and mix well. Drop by the teaspoon onto a lightly greased cookie sheet. Flatten gently with a fork. Bake 8-10 minutes at 350 degrees.

MILK-FREE ICE CREAM (my milk-tolerant husband prefers this to the real thing)
1 (8 oz.) container of Richwhip Topping, thawed (or any non-dairy equivalent frozen liquid whip topping)
1/4 cup sugar or equivalent sweetener
1 tsp. vanilla
Optional: 1 mashed banana, 1 cup of strawberries or blueberries or any favored fruit, fresh or frozen

Whip the topping as you would heavy cream. When thickened, add sugar, vanilla and fruit. Freeze for 1/2 hour. Remove from freezer and beat for one minute. Pour into storage container, cover and freeze. Natural it is not (read ingredients listed on topping carton), but delicious and milk-free it is!

HINT: If eggs are not on the sensitive list, add one to the above recipe. Separate the egg. Add yolk to thickened "cream" but beat the egg white till almost stiff before folding into mixture.

STRAWBERRY ICE
2 pkg. frozen sliced strawberries in syrup
1/3 cup ice water
1/4 cup orange juice, or omit water and use 3/4 cup orange juice
1/4 tsp. lemon juice

Spin together in an electric blender till smooth. Turn off, scrape sides, blend again and pour into a plastic container. Cover and freeze until serving time. Makes 4-6 servings. Let stand at room temperature 5 minutes or so if mixture has frozen hard. You may want to add 1/2 cup honey or sugar when using two pints of fresh berries.

Salton manufactures an electric ice cream machine that is excellent for making ices and milk-free ice cream-style desserts.

Even though it may seem at times that all products contain milk and all recipes demand it, this is not really so. **Here are some milk-free products that you'll be using:**

Meat, fish, poultry, eggs — prepared without milk products
All vegetables without butter or cream sauces
Potatoes (but not instant potatoes to which lactose has been added during processing)
Rice
Fruits (fresh, frozen or canned)
Chinese food (usually)
Kosher products, such as hot dogs (in kosher foods milk and meat are not combined)
Mayonnaise (such as Helmann's/Best Foods)
Pillsbury Crescent Rolls
Mazola Unsalted Margarine and some other diet brands
Pita Bread
Sourdough bread and authentic French Bread
Ry Krisp
Tortillas
Granola (not all brands)
Jams and jellies
Peanut butter
Carob
Campbell's Tomato Soup
Duncan Hines cake mixes (many of them)
Baskin Robbins Fruit Ice
Gelatin desserts
Cool Whip (although this contains sodium caseinate)
Hard candies
Popcorn (unbuttered)
Cracker Jacks
Juices
Triscuits and Ritz Crackers amongst others

In restaurants, fast food and otherwise, you'll not be able to let down your guard. Obviously you must avoid malts and shakes, but you must also watch out for creamed or breaded or batter dipped meat, fish or poultry. Also egg dishes made with milk, buttered vegetables, rolls and bread, salad dressings, creamed soups and chowders need to be avoided.

When your child goes to school or to a friend's house, send along a list to the person in charge of providing food, indicating what your child can have. This would include fruits, fruit juice, meat, raisins, nuts, raw vegetables. State specifically the foods with milk included that cannot be eaten: no milk, cheese, butter most margarines, yogurt (unless tolerated), ice cream, ice milk, sherbet, cakes, cookies, candy bars, hot dogs, etc.

Your pediatrician may suggest adding small amounts of milk to your child's menu periodically. If the symptoms reappear, refrain from serving milk for another few months.

To Market

A selective guide for parents

Shopping in a grocery store is a function performed by one, if not both parents, at least once a week. Each week we consider what we can get for our food dollar, what we can get in nutritional value, and what we can get that is appetizing both for ourselves and our families. There is no one in the grocery store to guide us through, or to tell us which foods meet each need we must give thought to. Much of the food in the grocery store has been placed there by food processors who derive large profits from their packaged edibles. It is necessary to shop armed with knowledge—and a calculator wouldn't hurt—to get the best buy for our money.

THE MOST HEALTHFUL WAY TO SHOP IN YOUR SUPERMARKET IS TO SHOP ONLY THE PERIPHERY OF THE STORE. The most wholesome and necessary foods are nearly all located in the outer aisles. There you will find dairy products, meats, produce, frozen foods, and probably the bakery area. Actually, you miss little by not going up and down the middle aisle, but we are conditioned to do this. Keep in mind that the dairy case is purposely set in the farthest corner to make sure you continue through the store.

The miracle of the modern distribution system is not convenience, as the major food companies would have you believe, but that you can eat bananas all year long that are grown in far away countries; that eggs are always available without your having to raise chickens; that those in the northern United States, where oranges don't grow and most crops are harvested in the fall, can eat fresh citrus fruit every day to insure adequate vitamin C intake. (You need vitamin C rich foods daily because your body cannot make its own vitamin C nor store it in appreciable amounts.)

Ideally, you should shop alone. Good luck! More often you are racing through the store before the baby awakens, or bribing your offspring to behave with food treats, or constantly berating them, "Do not touch. Stop running. No, you can't have that." Or is this the day your little one decides to have a tantrum in the grocery store? Do you recall your feelings as a teenager when you saw mothers "mishandle" their child's tantrum?

Why shop alone? So that you can read labels, compare prices, and not be coaxed into buying items you don't need. Since it is impractical to assume that you can do this all the time, it is important to do so every once in a while. I'm sure that it will have an invaluable carry-over when you must shop with tots in tow.

What should you look for when you do get a chance to read labels? Primarily SUGAR! Sugar listed as the first ingredient means that there is more sugar in that package than any other single ingredient. Try to buy products where sugar is specified at least third, if not fourth or fifth, on the label. This is not always significant however; while sugar might not be named first, you could find any of five additional sweeteners listed such as brown sugar, honey, molasses, dextrose and corn syrups. Food companies often combine the grains on labels but split the sugars, listing each type separately. Then sugar does not appear as the first ingredient.

Look to see where salt falls on the list of ingredients. The farther down the list, the better. While it is next to impossible to avoid salt, you will at least see why nutritionists and doctors are so concerned about our excessive salt consumption. You might be spurred to make more dishes from scratch without salt when you realize how abundantly it is used in packaged foods. It is in diet soft drinks, canned tuna, canned vegetables, mayonnaise (list of ingredients not required) and grated Parmesan cheese, to name a few.

Choose, when possible, "enriched white flour" over "flour". The latter is often listed as "wheat flour".

Also try to avoid hardened (hydrogenated) fats. They are harder to digest.

Choose natural flavorings over artificial flavorings whenever possible. Generally, the fewer chemical additives in food the better off you will be. Natural flavorings are often more expensive than artificial (synthetic) ones, which is why they are less commonly used. Food colorings (found most frequently in soda, candy, gelatin mixes, pudding mixes, cereals, ice cream and other snack foods) are needed in manufactured foods to imply richness and flavor to the eye. While most additives are safe, they do make less wholesome foods appear more wholesome and appetizing.

Let's take a short trip down grocery store lane rethinking what we see there every week, looking for the best in food value, particularly for the small children in our households. If your favorite foods are skipped over. forgive me. Some have been skipped on purpose; others not.

Produce

Let's start with the produce section, usually near the entrance anyway. (And produce always gets squished on the bottom of the basket, too.)

Bananas

> When you buy them green, wait until they are yellow and ripe before eating. Bananas can be bought on special (which means they are ripe) and used for banana bread, milk shakes or popsicles. You can mash and freeze them for later baking uses. Usually 3 bananas equal one pound.

Apples

> One of the best fall, winter and spring fruits which most children enjoy. They are good plain, baked, dried and sauced. Try serving half-an-apple on a popsicle stick. The best gadget I ever purchased is an apple corer that removes the center easily, going a long way to eliminate waste by children who never eat close to the core. And there is an apple cutter on the market that cuts an apple into eight sections with one downward push.

Oranges

> While squeeze-it-yourself orange juice is certainly best because the pulp also provides important food value. You may opt for the frozen variety since it is inexpensive, convenient, and there is no sugar added. To provide the food value of the pulp, do serve eating oranges regularly. Navel oranges have few or no seeds. Instead of slicing them in quarters, for a change cut them in 1/4 inch slices so you have orange circles. Oranges are often artificially colored so don't be put off by oranges with a green tinge. They are fine!

Pears

Follow pretty much the application for apples. If they are too firm when you buy them, let them sit on your counter a few days to soften, then refrigerate.

Peaches

Look for good peach tones, not green tones, when peaches are in season.

Cantaloupe

This summer fruit is tops in taste and food value. A ripe cantaloupe usually smells as good as it tastes, which is usually at the height of its season when it is most plentiful. Serve it wedged or cubed, morning or night.

Watermelon

This summer fruit is another good-for-you melon. For ripeness, look for a flattish yellow side. Young children usually like (or need) pits removed. If you cube it, remove the pits. Whir it in a blender and then freeze it in popsicle forms for a treat. Best served outdoors, as it's so drippy.

Berries

These were invented just the right size for children and most children love them. Serve with toothpicks, or in cream, or combined with other fruits.

Grapes

Green seedless are favored by most. You may want to cut them in half for very young children to insure that they are eaten and not just swallowed whole. A small plastic bag is a good container for a bunch of grapes.

Pineapple

Should smell as fresh as it looks. There should be a yellow blush on the skin, and the leaves should be dark green.

Carrots

Unless they are very scruffy looking, carrots need not be peeled. A good scrub is sufficient. If you puree them for an infant, peel to remove bacteria or insect parts which might hang on. Carrots are more digestible when they are cooked soft, though children as they grow older tend to prefer carrots raw. Short on time? Slice them before cooking.

Cucumbers

Usually waxed for transporting so you may wish to use your carrot peeler here. The largest ones don't always taste the best. If you grow your own, do leave the green skin on. If you need to remove the seeds to have them eaten, do so.

Potatoes

White potatoes are rich in minerals and vitamins, including vitamin C. A medium-sized potato has about the same number of calories as a large apple. Potatoes baked or boiled in their jackets are more nutritious than French-fried. Sweet potatoes and yams offer the same plus a lot of vitamin A and more fiber. No potato, white or yellow, should be stored in the refrigerator as the excess coolness can change its texture.

ST. PATRICK'S POTATOES

Combine mashed potatoes, pureed broccoli, a bit of milk and grated Parmesan cheese.

Lettuces

All varieties may not be preferred but they are all a good source of fiber.

Tomatoes

Slice for sandwiches and salads. Use for liquid in stews and sauces, straining out seeds.

Green vegetables

Broccoli, asparagus, zucchini, etc.—all of which are excellent for you. (My son won't touch any green vegetables with the exception of artichokes dipped in butter sauce.) Most can be served raw with a dip as well as steamed or baked.

This could continue but I'll stop here so we may move on through the "store."

In Cans and Jars

Applesauce

Motts, for one, puts out a natural style applesauce which contains apples and water only. It is found in the same section as applesauces which contain added sugar, and sometimes salt and citric acid. Do check. Natural applesauce is priced higher but it is a better buy.

Try to select canned fruits packed in light syrup rather than heavy. Heavy syrup means heavy with sugar. Light syrup has less sugar. Some fruits are packed in their own juice without extra sugar added.

Tuna fish

Probably our most popular canned fish. The kind of fish that goes into the can varies and so does the price. The term "white meat" designates the whitest, fanciest and most expensive. "Light meat" is a combination of fish similar in color and flavor that serves as a versatile all purpose choice for less money. Solid packs cost more because they consist of more pieces. Chunked tuna in smaller pieces costs less and still cheaper is flaked or grated, all fine for sandwiches or casseroles. Supermarket or private brands or unadvertised brands are usually cheaper and sometimes just as nutritious as advertised brands. (Who do you suppose makes the private brands? In many cases the same company that makes the advertised brands!)

Peanut butter

It supplies protein, carbohydrates and vegetable fat—all necessary for good growth and energy. Shelf-stable peanut butter (all those nationally advertised brands and maybe even a store brand) is so-called because of all the extras that go into the jar. The first added ingredient you will note is sugar (sometimes listed as dextrose) to make the product palatable (and possibly to mask inferior peanuts), as though it weren't good tasting enough by itself. But mainly you will find hydrogenated oil. This is a heavy oil, hard to digest, which gives peanut butter its uniform spreading quality. It also prevents the oil from separating and rising to the top of the jar. You can find top quality peanut butter consisting of just peanuts and a dash of salt in your grocery's refrigerated section. It is well worth the extra money. Natural brands are also appearing on the shelf. These simply need a quick stir before refrigerating to keep the oil mixed.

Make your own, if you are ambitious. Shell your own peanuts and put a cupful in a blender with a tablespoon of oil—and there you have it! Or you can cheat as I do and buy bags of shelled peanuts to work with . . . I should add that peanuts that come shelled often are treated to preserve their freshness. The shell does the same thing naturally.

HINT: 7 Tbsp. of peanut butter equal a 1/2 cup of peanut butter. Oil spoon or measuring cup before measuring.

Breakfast Cereals

Many cereals that children eat are heavily sugared and heavily fortified, making them basically a sugar-coated vitamin candy in a cereal bowl rather than a natural food of good fiber. Breakfasting on them is really not a good way to start the day. Avoid those with sugar listed on the package as a first ingredient and if possible, second or third. Of course children will eat them; they taste good, being mainly sugar! If your kids want only King Vitamin/Sugar Smacks or Cocoa Pebbles, and you think that Shredded Wheat and wheat germ are preferable, maybe a middle-of-the-road choice such as Life, Wheaties, Corn Flakes, Cheerios or Rice Krispies would be agreeable. You can enrich any breakfast cereal by adding toasted wheat germ to it.

There are many nutritious hot cereals, though I have never been able to con my kids into eating them. Mine prefer cold whole grain cereals such as granola. While granola is high in calories, owing to the honey and oil used, it is high in natural fiber and nutritional ingredients, and you won't find a list of additives on the package. Incidentally, Quaker 100% Natural and Kretschmer's Sun Country are two granolas to which salt has not been added.

To make your own, check out page 94. It's surprisingly easy.

Also serve cereal in a mug with a handle for a change of pace. A new container gives an old regular fresh appeal.

Sucrose and Glucose Content of Commercially Available Breakfast Cereals

Commercial Cereal Product	Sucrose Content (%)	Glucose Content (%)	Commercial Cereal Product	(%) Sucrose Content	Glucose Content (%)
SHREDDED WHEAT (large biscuit)	1.0	0.2	ALL BRAN	20.0	1.6
SHREDDED WHEAT (spoon size biscuit)	1.3	0.3	GRANOLA (with almonds and filberts)	21.4	1.2
CHEERIOS	2.2	0.5	FORTIFIED OAT FLAKES	22.2	1.2
PUFFED RICE	2.4	0.4	HEARTLAND	23.1	3.2
UNCLE SAM CEREAL	2.4	1.2	SUPER SUGAR CHEX	24.5	0.8
WHEAT CHEX	2.6	0.9	SUGAR FROSTED FLAKES	29.0	1.8
GRAPE NUT FLAKES	3.3	0.6	BRAN BUDS	30.2	2.1
PUFFED WHEAT	3.5	0.7	SUGAR SPARKLED CORN FLAKES	32.2	1.8
ALPEN	3.8	4.7	FROSTED MINI WHEATS	33.6	0.4
POST TOASTIES	4.1	1.7	SUGAR POPS	37.8	2.9
PRODUCT 19	4.1	1.7	ALPHA BITS	40.3	0.6
CORN TOTAL	4.4	1.4	SIR GRAPEFELLOW	40.7	3.1
SPECIAL K	4.4	6.4	SUPER SUGAR CRISP	40.7	4.5
WHEATIES	4.7	4.2	COCOA PUFFS	43.0	3.5
CORN FLAKES (Kroger)	5.1	1.5	CAP'N CRUNCH	43.3	0.8
PEANUT BUTTER	5.2	1.1	CRUNCH BERRIES	43.4	1.0
GRAPE NUTS	6.6	1.1	KABOOM	43.8	3.0
CORN FLAKES (Food Club)	7.0	2.1	FRANKENBERRY	44.0	2.6
CRISPY RICE	7.3	1.5	FROSTED FLAKES	44.0	2.9
CORN CHEX	7.5	0.9	COUNT CHOCULA	44.2	3.7
CORN FLAKES (Kellogg)	7.8	6.4	ORANGE QUANGAROOS	44.7	0.6
TOTAL	8.1	1.3	QUISP	44.9	0.6
RICE CHEX	8.5	1.8	BOO BERRY	45.7	2.8
CRISP RICE	8.8	2.1	VANILLY CRUNCH	45.8	0.7
RAISIN BRAN (Skinner)	9.6	9.3	BARON VON REDBERRY	45.8	1.5
CONCENTRATE	9.9	2.4	COCOA KRISPIES	45.9	0.8
RICE CRISPIES (Kellogg)	10.0	2.9	TRIX	46.6	4.1
RAISIN BRAN (Kellogg)	10.6	14.1	FROOT LOOPS	47.4	0.5
HEARTLAND (with raisins)	13.5	5.6	HONEYCOMB	48.8	2.8
BUCK WHEAT	13.6	1.5	PINK PANTHER	49.2	1.3
LIFE	14.5	2.5	CINNAMON CRUNCH	50.3	3.2
GRANOLA (with dates)	14.5	3.2	LUCKY CHARMS	50.4	7.6
GRANOLA (with raisins)	14.5	3.8	COCOA PEBBLES	53.5	0.6
SUGAR FROSTED CORN FLAKES	15.6	1.8	APPLE JACKS	55.0	0.5
40% BRAN FLAKES (Post)	15.8	3.0	FRUITY PEBBLES	55.1	1.1
TEAM	15.9	1.1	KING VITAMAN	58.5	3.1
BROWN SUGAR-CINNAMON FROSTED MINI WHEATS	16.0	0.3	SUGAR SMACKS	61.3	2.4
40% BRAN FLAKES (Kellogg)	16.2	2.1	SUPER ORANGE CRISP	68.0	2.8
GRANOLA	16.6	0.6	MEAN	25.1	2.3
100% BRAN	18.4	0.8	S. D.	19.16	2.21

White Flour

When buying flour, you will probably choose between regular white flour and whole wheat flour (see page 124 for additional information). If you purchase white flour, unbleached is preferable. Unbleached simply means that it has gone through one less processing stage which is done for appearance (whitening) only. Once you find the word "unbleached" on the label, look for "enriched." This means that niacin, thiamin, riboflavin and iron have been put back. But this is a replacement of only a few of the many nutrients that have been milled out. So if you are using only white flour and have not yet expanded your horizons, do make sure that you at least purchase the kind which has been enriched. When flour, or any product, is enriched beyond its original level of nutrients, it is—must be—labeled "fortified."

In reading labels you will notice that everything from pretzels to tomato soup seems to contain flour. Sometimes the flour is enriched, sometimes not. Given a choice between similar products, do buy the one with enriched flour. Sometimes white flour is referred to on labels as wheat flour, which it is. This doesn't mean enriched or whole wheat, just white flour! Don't be deceived.

There is a terrific way to enrich the white flour you use that won't change its texture or taste, but will put back most of what is left out. Notice that we said enriched, not fortified. It is called the CORNELL TRIPLE RICH FORMULA. Though not a new idea, it is not a commonly used idea—which it should be.

Before putting any flour into your measuring cup, place in the bottom of your one cup measure:

    1 Tbsp. soy flour
    1 Tbsp. powdered dry milk
    1 tsp. regular wheat germ (not the toasted variety)
Then add flour to complete one cup. Mix well. Do this for each cup of flour used. Even whole grain flour benefits from this formula.

To make this even easier for yourself, combine the above three ingredients in the same proportions in a large jar and store it in your refrigerator. Then when you need anything enriched, simply take two or three spoonfuls from the jar for each cup of flour and spare yourself opening three containers each time.

You'll notice we said to refrigerate this. That is because soy flour (you may have to go to a health food store or co-op to find this) and wheat germ need refrigeration to prevent them from turning rancid. While dry milk does not become rancid (no need to refrigerate) it can go stale. For this reason, I prefer to buy dry milk that comes in envelopes within a box. If you use lots of dry milk and can go through a box in a month, there is no need to bother with the more expensive packaged "envelope-in-the-box" variety.

Remember that this Triple Rich Formula can be used in everything you bake that uses flour: cookies, cakes, breads, waffles, muffins, pancakes, pie-crusts, even some mixes if used in moderation. Try to make it a habit.

Whole Wheat Flour

If you wish to buy completely and naturally enriched flour, buy whole wheat. You may want to purchase whole wheat flour that has been "stone ground." This means that the whole wheat kernel has been crushed into a fine flour in one process. Absence of the phrase "stone ground whole wheat flour" from the label indicates that the kernel has been milled as for white flour. The bran, wheat germ and center flour kernel were separated and then remixed in proper proportion to give you whole wheat flour. This makes a lighter whole wheat flour but the heat from the extra milling processes destroys many extra nutrients. It still beats white flour on the food value scale, however.

Whole wheat flour really has a very limited shelf life. Millers expect it to go stale in two to three months, rancid in a year. Oil in the wheat germ is the spoiler. Millers and grocers make a great effort to ensure that the whole wheat flour you buy in the grocery store is as fresh as possible. Once you get it home, store it in your refrigerator or freezer unless you expect to use it up promptly.

Interestingly enough, the whole wheat flour and white flour available to us in the grocery are made from two different types of wheat. Whole wheat flour comes from a variety that is 14-15 percent protein, while our commercial white flour comes from a brand that is 11 percent protein. When the outer bran and wheat germ are milled out of this second type, the resulting white flour has approximately 10 percent protein. Bran and wheat germ are removed so that this lower protein white flour will be a better textured product for baking breads and pastries and have a longer shelf life.

There is a whole wheat pastry flour (that is usually only found in health food stores) that is made from a softer whole wheat and is similar in texture to white flour. It works well in crusts, bars, cookies, and other such items. It will not rise in yeast breads. If you object to the coarsness of regular whole wheat flour, you may want to experiment here.

Wheat Germ

Wheat germ, which can usually be found in the cereal section of your grocery store, is a super food. If you don't like to use it by itself, use it to sneak extra good nutrition into foods your family normally eats. Wheat germ, you will notice, comes two ways— regular and toasted. I buy both. The regular variety is good for use in the Cornell Triple Rich Formula, granola, meat loaf (like bread crumbs), and for enriching innumerable other recipes. Toasted wheat germ, which also works well in granola, is good for toppings also, mixed with chopped peanuts, and sprinkled in sandwiches or salads or wherever you like a sweet and nutty topping. The toasted kind is toasted with honey or sugar, making it more palatable. Wheat germ provides a variety of vitamin B's that you could be missing from your diet, especially if you don't eat whole grain breads, yogurt, liver or nutritional brewer's yeast. Wheat germ is so easy to add to foods without detection. And remember, it must be refrigerated.

Buying Bread

If you and your family are hooked on plain white bread, switching will not be easy. First, of course, you must believe that the switch is worthwhile. It takes some effort to read labels and can cost more (good ingredients are more expensive). Look for breads which include whole grains among the primary ingredients. Check the label for caramel coloring because some breads are made with it to look like whole grain breads when they are not. Also, make the switch gradually. Experiment until you find a bread you can live with. Because whole grain breads are more filling, you may not need to buy as much bread and the cost can equal out. You will notice this when you make sure you are buying bread by weight and not size. Breads made with milk, whole or powdered, supply added nutrients.

An interesting bread available in some grocery stores is called "Pita bread." It is also known as "pocket bread" or "Syrian flat bread." This is bread dough shaped in a flat circle. When baked it provides a hidden pocket between the thin crusts. It is available as whole wheat or white bread. It is a low calorie bread containing no fats, no shortening and no preservatives. Some stores carry it in their refrigerated bread sections; others, in the freezer bread section. Most anything can be stuffed in the pockets when the bread is cut in half: sloppy Joes, taco filling, hamburger, pizza makings, deli-meats, chili, sausage and onions, scrambled eggs and bacon—you name it! When split open they make a good crust for an individual pizza.

Adventurous? . . . try to make your own:

Pita Bread
    1 pkg. yeast
    1-1/4 cup lukewarm water
    3 cups flour (white, whole wheat or any combination)
    2 tsp. salt
Dissolve yeast in the lukewarm water. Stir in flour and salt. Stir into a rough sticky ball. Knead on floured board until smooth, adding more flour if necessary.

Divide into six balls and knead each ball until smooth and round. With a rolling pin, flatten each until 1/4 inch thick and about four or five inches in diameter.

Cover with a towel and let rise 45 minutes. Arrange the rounds upside down on baking sheets. Bake in a very hot oven (500 degrees) for 10-15 minutes or until browned and puffed in the center.

The breads will be hard when they are removed from the oven, but will soften and flatten as they cool. For sandwiches, split carefully and fill with any combination of sandwich makings.

Oatmeal

Oatmeal processed as rolled oats is a popular grain that is probably better liked in cookies than in the cereal bowl. It contains much good food value in whatever form it is eaten. Oatmeal contains the bran and the germ of the oat, and little nutritional value is lost when it is milled in the rolling process. It also provides good fiber. The steel cut variety is the most nutritious but it requires an hour to cook. Its slightly less nutritious cousin, known as "old fashioned" oats, cooks up in five minutes. Avoid the one minute kind as extra food value is eliminated during its manufacture. Oatmeal is terrific in cookies, bars, breads, granolas, toppings and, yes, even as a bowl of hot cereal.

Cookies

Walking down the cookie aisle, which always seems to be next to the candy section, is usually an ordeal with children along. My basic approach to buying commercial cookies (if and when I do) is to choose those with redeeming value having fillings such as peanut butter, figs, dates, etc., or to buy cookies made with whole grain flours or oatmeal as their major ingredients.

Did you know that graham crackers with different but similar names on their boxes have different proportionate ingredients? Following is a list of three kinds of Nabisco Graham Crackers and the order of ingredients listed on their boxes:

Cinnamon Treats: Enriched wheat flour, sugar, shortening, graham flour, rye flour, corn sweeteners, honey, molasses, salt, leavening and cinnamon.

Honey Maid: Enriched wheat flour, sugar, shortening, graham flour, rye flour, honey, corn sweeteners, salt, leavening and artificial flavor.

Graham Crackers: Enriched wheat flour, graham flour, rye flour, sugar, shortening, molasses, corn sweeteners, salt and leavening.

I don't know about you, but I would certainly vote for the last one. Also, here is an instance where the wheat flour mentioned refers to white flour and not whole wheat flour.

Cream-filled cookies are usually highest in sugar. Pepperidge Farm cookies, while expensive, are made with good quality ingredients. Their Short Bread Cookies and Date Nut Granola Cookies are relatively low in sugar content. All Pepperidge Farm cookies contain no artificial colorings, flavorings or preservatives. This is not true of most cookie manufacturers.

Crackers

I think that generally crackers can be a good substitute for cookies if you stay away from the heavily salted kind. The variety in stores is large (though crackers are seldom confined to one area). Check them out! Melba-toast, Stoned Wheat Thins, even snack crackers tend to provide a good variety of grain flours and much less sugar.

Ritz Crackers have less sugar than cookies but are not sugar-free. Saltines are sugar-free but not salt-free. Of the saltines, Premium brand contains the least salt, as indicated by a comparison of box labels.

Commercial Baby Food

Commercial baby foods are under attack for many good reasons. Several things added to commercial baby foods—sugar, salt, modified starches, for example—are considered by many experts as unnecessary! These ingredients raise the caloric content and the price and can condition baby's taste buds early. Such prepared foods do not provide your baby, penny for penny, what you could easily prepare yourself. Unless percentage labeling is provided you cannot be sure how much you are paying for strained carrots and how much you are paying for their jar, their water, to say nothing of their advertising and your "convenience." (It's about half the price to make your own.)

Commercial baby foods are often high in water content and low in solid content. The foods appear solid because tapioca and modified starches are added as thickeners. Digestibility of modified starches by babies is debatable. The starches are not harmful but they may limit absorption of nutritional values. A jar may contain 60 percent fruit and 40 percent water thickened to look uniform throughout. Avoid paying fruit and vegetable prices for modified starches and water. The added sugar in baby foods—aimed at Mom's taste buds, primarily—results in early development of a sweet tooth, contributing to future obesity and tooth decay. Avoid baby juices with added sugar. Remember that regular unsweetened apple juice is already "strained."

Salt is probably the most worrisome ingredient added to baby foods. Salt is believed by many to add significantly to the possibility of hypertension in later life, especially when there is such a tendency in the family. When you prepare your own baby foods, do so without the use of flavor enhancers such as salt. It is encouraging that commercial baby food manufacturers have now removed salt from their jars, and sugar from many others.

Most of us use commercial baby foods at times. How does one pick and choose from the vast array of products? First, remember that most doctors today agree that until they are four to six months of age babies do not need solid foods. Mother's milk or formula provides everything most full-term babies need until then. Cereal is a good first food because it is a good source of iron. Iron is low in mother's milk and in the regular formula you buy ready-to-feed. The American Academy of Pediatrics now recommends iron-fortified formula for babies from two to 12 months old. When the time comes to use pureed foods and you are not making your own, choose from single basic fruits, vegetables and meats. Avoid sugar, salt and modified starches whenever possible.

Avoid completely baby food desserts, combination dinners and foods that you can buy better and cheaper in their natural state elsewhere in the grocery store. For example, mash your own banana (and talk about a good container, it's even unbreakable if dropped) instead of buying strained bananas. Other good "baby foods" to be found elsewhere in the store are:

    Unsweetened applesauce
    Yogurt
    Cottage cheese
    Cooked eggs (yolk only till the baby is eight months old)
    Baked potato
    Sweet potato
    Squash
    Pumpkin
    Hot cereals you cook yourself

It is important to get your babies off to a good start while you have total control of their dietary intake.

Dairy

There is skim milk, regular milk and milks with varying butterfat content. All are fortified with vitamins A and D. So milk is a good source of some vitamins and calcium and—remember this— **a lot of protein!** One percent milk has 1 percent butterfat; two percent milk has 2 percent butterfat; and whole milk has 3-1/4 percent butterfat. Skim milk is exactly the same as other milk but without any butterfat. Since our diets tend to be fat-laden enough, skim milk is probably best for all of us. You will find that opinions vary here. The main exception is under the age of two years. If they need to cut back on calories, do it elsewhere, not here. That extra butterfat is important to early growth and development.

Powdered non-fat dry milk is an economical way to purchase milk. You reconstitute it yourself. The most frequent complaint is that it tastes like it has been reconstituted. To avoid this, mix the reconstituted powdered milk in a blender and let it stand in the refrigerator at least 12 hours before using. At the very least you can use reconstituted milk when cooking and baking.

Yogurt

Yogurt has the dubious distinction of being an excellent food with the worst of all possible names. Despite this handicap, and that of being considered a "health food," it has made its mark upon the dairy sections all over the country.

Yogurt is milk cultured by live bacteria. In fact, without bacteria it really isn't yogurt. There is no federal standard for yogurt so bacteria counts vary. All ingredients are listed on the container. The common base ingredient is cultured lowfat milk, and milk or skim milk solids. Different companies add different "thickeners" to their products. Some companies add gelatin. Others add modified food starch, citric acid, sodium caseinate. Avoid these latter additives when possible. Despite the fact that it is made with lowfat milk solids, there are 150 calories in a container of plain yogurt; over 200 calories in the fruited kind.

There are all those yummy flavors. Unfortunately, most are made up of artificial colorings and flavorings and added sugar. Some companies even pasteurize yogurt which kills off all the bacteria—and bacteria is what yogurt is all about.

Dannon Yogurt, although not yet nationally distributed, is reputed to be one of the best tasting yogurts around. It contains all natural ingredients and has a high bacteria count. Others well rated are Columbo, Yami and Lacto. If you are not bothering to check labels, most fancy flavored commercial yogurts should be viewed as a better-for-you, high-caloried dairy treat rather than for its value as a cultured yogurt. But that still leaves it providing a lot of protein and calcium. The frozen yogurts also lose their bacteria value through freezing but they still have 1/2 the calories of regular ice cream.

Plain yogurt combines well with many foods, if you don't enjoy it plain. It can be used:

- as a popsicle base
- combined with fresh fruits
- mixed with tuna or clams for a dip
- combined with ricotta cheese when making Lasagne
- substituted for milk in souffles or omlettes
- instead of sour cream
- as a topping for pies or pancakes
- as a salad dressing (see page 36)

Eggs
Eggs are a terrific food. All sorts of good nutrients lie packaged in that well-designed shell. On a cost per serving basis it is most inexpensive. If there is less than a 7 cent price spread between one size and the next, buy the largest size.

To tell if an egg in the shell is raw or hard-cooked, spin it on a flat surface. If it spins fast and easily, it is hard-cooked. If it wobbles, it's raw.

Egg's high cholesterol count makes it a controversial food. Information and studies coming to light these days imply that dietary reduction of cholesterol intake might not affect our body build-up of cholesterol. Perhaps a more important factor regarding cholesterol build-up is the consumption of all the other refined foods we eat. Our body manufactures cholesterol and ingestion of foods high in cholesterol may not be the culprit we thought. Information is still not conclusive. Exercise is a factor. By all means, listen to your doctor if he is limiting your cholesterol intake.

If you have run out of ideas on new ways to entice your children to eat eggs when you are serving them, may I suggest:

GREEN EGGS AND HAM

> Beat one or two eggs well and add a drop or two of **blue** food coloring before cooking in a pan. Add a slice (or cubes) of left over ham. Dr. Suess will love you for it!

Cheese

Have you ever noticed that Kraft's package of 32 slices of American cheese comes two ways? For the same price you can buy it with slices individually wrapped or not. So what is the difference? How can a package requiring that much additional wrapping be the same price? Well, it can't and the difference is written on the front of the package. One says "AMERICAN-PASTEURIZED PROCESS CHEESE FOOD" and the other "AMERICAN PASTEUR-IZED PROCESSED AMERICAN CHEESE," a significant difference in that **cheese food** is made of less cheese and more water. It's right on the front label, yet our "mental set" for convenience lets us overlook what is right in front of our noses.

Cheeses are a readily available source of calcium and protein, usually well received, good for rapidly growing children. Hard and natural cheeses are a better food value than processed cheeses. Processed cheeses cost less, have more additives and are processed with water; ergo, you pay for higher water content. Natural cheeses are made from milk solids. Natural cheeses in hunks will give you your best dollar buy. The sharper the flavor of cheese the higher the price. Domestic cheeses tend to be less expensive than imported ones.

Cream cheese, I'm sorry to say, is not really a good source of protein. It offers more in fat than in protein value. Therefore, do try to serve it with something more nourishing than jelly, such as peanut butter, meats or sun flower seeds. A tablespoon of powdered milk added to one 8 ounce package of cream cheese is a good enrichment idea.

Beverages

Any canned beverage which says "DRINK" or "-ADE" on the label is telling you that you are buying mainly water. No doubt the next ingredient is sugar followed by artificial flavorings and colorings. The manufacturer might even throw in some real juice. If you buy these drinks at about 35 cents a can, you may get one-tenth of a quart of fruit juice. That means that you have to buy 10 cans to get one whole quart of 100 percent juice. Just think, you are paying $3.50 a quart to get fruit juice. If you really don't care about the juice, why not just add sugar to your own water and throw in some artificial colorings and flavorings?

When you buy the real thing—fruit juice, that is—you are getting a bargain because all the vitamins, minerals and natural fruit carbohydrates (versus refined sugar) are present at no extra cost. A label will state "pure fruit juice." If it says "juice" only, then it may be but 50 percent juice. If it says "drink," then it will be no more than 10 percent juice. Apple juice (and make sure that the label does not say "added sugar") and grape juice are two favorite no-sugar-added juices available in bottles. (The frozen grape juice concentrate in cans does have some sugar added while grape juice in bottles does not.)

If you need to stretch your own fruit juice, do so by adding five parts water to one part fresh fruit juice. Add sweetener to taste.

As for Tang, here is a list of the ingredients found on the label: sugar, citric acid, calcium phosphate (regulates tartness and prevents caking), modified starches (provides body), natural orange flavoring, vitamin C, hydrogenated coconut oil, artificial flavor, artificial color, vitamin A palmitate, BHA. Since your water and their vitamin C are the major good food values in Tang, why not just serve a vitamin C tablet with a glass of water?

When purchasing carbonated sodas, do remember that again you are buying water, bubbles, sugar, colorings and flavorings. Granted they taste good, but they provide a tremendous amount of calories and no nutritional benefit. For the most part, clear type diet drinks such as the lemon and lime type and 7-UP (regular and sugar-free) tend to use no artificial colorings and flavorings. Read the labels. It's all written out for you.

Dr. Pepper and other cola drinks contain caffeine. One large-size bottle of a drink such as Dr. Pepper provides a child with as much as half the caffeine you have in your cup of coffee. A glass of ginger ale contains six to eight teaspoons of sugar. You would not put that much sugar in your own coffee or tea and yet these beverages are served to our children without a second thought.

My personal inclination has been toward sugar-free beverages but even these are regarded as a treat and not as a staple. Let's remember that the reason we drink is to quench our thirst and not to add empty calories to our dietary intake. That brings us back to clear, sparkling, splendid . . . WATER! And it's on tap.

Hot Dogs

Just a few words about hot dogs. They have come under attack recently owing to the inclusion of sodium nitrites, a questionable additive also used in many luncheon meats, ham and other cured meat products. This additive prevents botulism (food poisoning) and gives a reddish color to the products it's used in.

Nitrites in large doses can be toxic but they are used in very, very small quantities in hot dogs as a preservative and coloring agent. Nitrites and nitrates occur naturally in many foods we eat. Most green vegetables (lettuce, spinach) contain nitrates in higher amounts than is allowed as additives to foods. The concern is not about the nitrites themselves but because they can form nitrosamines which in large amounts have proved to be cancer-causing.

Confusing? Even the experts trying to determine the safety of this additive are divided on the issue. Rather than putting on blinders (Oh, no, another food I can't eat! Who are they kidding? I'll just forget it!), I think it is reasonable to limit our consumption of foods containing sodium nitrite. Hot dogs once a week, I think, are not a problem. However, bacon for breakfast, hot dogs for lunch, ham for dinner and beef jerky for snacks might well constitute one. A better reason to avoid serving hot dogs is their high fat content. The average hot dog is 29 percent fat by weight, and high fat content in the American diet contributes to heart disease —the number one cause of death in the United States.

Freezer Section

The freezer section of the supermarket is part of today's miracle. Still, as everywhere else in the store, selective shopping is the key. Some best buys for food value in the frozen foods section are:

> Frozen orange juice concentrate
> Frozen sugarless apple juice concentrate
> Frozen vegetables in large transparent bags
> Fish (and I do not mean fish sticks)
> Turkey
> Frozen fruits (packed without sugar)
> Frozen whole wheat bread dough
> Quality ice creams made with natural ingredients and
>   cream (not milk)

Well, enough of our trip through the grocery store. I certainly did not cover everything but I have tried to touch on foods that, those of us with small children, gravitate towards. For a much more complete guide, I recommend "THE SUPERMARKET HAND-BOOK" by Nikki and David Goldbeck (Signet, 1974), $1.98.

As I look back over my comments I see that I often mention products that could cost you more. I don't think that buying better will cost you less but I don't believe it has to cost you more, either. When you buy apple juice instead of soda pop, peanut butter with natural ingredients versus luncheon meats, a hunk of cheese instead of two packages of chips, you will probably come out the same. Your variety may not be quite as wide as in the past but the quality will certainly be better.

And speaking of money, a few last words about living within a budget at the grocery store. I don't know whether it is really possible. Articles I've read about folks who pass on such information in women's magazines (usually the family of eight is living on $50 worth of monthly groceries) has never translated well for me. In fact, I find that a neighborhood grocery store which provides the most economical buys for one of my neighbors doesn't do so for me. It all depends on what you intend to buy, and only you can do a cost comparison on that.

As for grocery store coupons, they may save you money, but beware! Do you realize that only a small portion of them ever offers values on basic foods? They are usually offered on convenience and packaged foods and non-food products (thanks to the manufacturers) rather than on your meats, produce and dairy items.

While waiting in the check-out line you can always play my favorite supermarket game "What's Your Bag?" Just casually eye the contents of the grocery cart next to yours. Try not to be obvious; you don't want to appear nosey. There's a lot you can learn about the life style of other shoppers. Do they have a large family or are they single? Do they own a dog or a cat? Do they entertain lavishly or frugally? But, more important, can you size up their nutrition consciousness? Do you see whole grain or white flour products? Fresh produce or canned goods? Cans of soda pop, fruit drinks or juice? Candy bars or dried fruit snacks? This is a very revealing "game." Remember that the next time you notice someone eyeing your grocery cart.

DESSERT: THE REASON FOR EATING A MEAL.

Contemporary Glossary of Kitchen Terms

APPETIZING

anything advertised on TV

APPLE

tooth fairy's delight

BANANAS

tropical disease which affects a parent as a child swings into 6th month of a food jag

BOIL

a point parents reach when hearing the automatic "yuk" before food is even tasted

CASSEROLE

a combination of favorite foods that go uneaten because they are mixed together

CHAIR

spot left vacant by mid-meal bathroom visit

CONCESSION

a C.A.N.D.Y. stand where a parent usually concedes

COOKIE(last one)

an item that must be eaten in front of a sibling

CRUST	the part of a sandwich saved for the starving children of (check one): China, India, Africa or Europe
DESSERT	the reason for eating a meal
EVAPORATE	magic trick performed by children when it comes time to clear the table or wash the dishes
FAT	microscopic substance detected visually by children on pieces of meat they do not wish to eat
FIBER	nutrient found out-of-doors, such as in the sandbox
FISH	a form of protein with "too many bones"
FLOOR	place for all food not found on lap or seat
FORK	eating utensil made obsolete by the discovery of fingers
FRIED FOODS	gourmet cooking to kids
FROZEN	condition of children's jaws when spinach is served
FRUIT	a natural sweet not to be confused with dessert
GERMS	the only thing kids will share freely
HUNGRY	constant condition of both well-nourished and mal-nourished children
JELLY BEAN	the only "vegetable" all kids will eat
JUICE	a football star who also runs through airports
KETCHUP	a condiment that other foods are eaten with

KITCHEN	the only room not used when eating a crumbly snack
LEFTOVERS	commonly described as "gross"
LIVER	a food that affects genes creating a hereditary dislike
LOLLIPOP	a snack provided by people who don't have to pay your dental bills
MAPLE	a tree that has given its name to an artificially flavored syrup
METRIC	a system of measurement that will be accepted only after 40 years of wandering in the desert
MEASURING CUP	a kitchen utensil which is stored in the sandbox
MILK	a widely used floor cleaner
NATURAL FOOD	food eaten with unwashed hands
NUTRITION	a secret war waged by parents using direct commands, camouflage and constant guard duty
NAPKIN	any worn cloth object, such as shirt or pants
MACARONI	material for a collage
PEANUT BUTTER	staff of life
PLATE	breakable Frisbee
POT LUCK	when children set the table

REFRIGERATOR	a very expensive and inefficient room air conditioner
SALIVA	a medium for blowing bubbles
SODA POP	Shake 'n Spray
SUCKER	a parent who lets kids eat dessert who haven't finished their main meal
SNACK	the meal lasting all day
TABLE	a place for storing gum
TABLE LEG	a percussion instrument
THIRSTY	how your child feels after you've said your final "good night"
UNSTICK	when a fast melting popsicle departs from its stick
VEGETABLE	a basic food known to satisfy kids' hunger . . . but only by sight!
WATER	popular beverage in underdeveloped countries
YUKKY	half of the vocabulary of a child
YUMMY	other half of vocabulary of same child

FOOD EQUIVALENTS FOR MILK

1 cup buttermilk	=	1 cup milk
1 cup yogurt	=	1 cup milk
1/2 cup ice cream	=	1/4 cup milk
1/2 cup ice milk	=	1/3 cup milk
1 cup baked custard	=	1 cup milk
1 oz. (slice) Swiss cheese	=	1 cup milk
1 slice Am Proc. cheese	=	1/2 cup milk
1 inch cube Cheddar cheese	=	1/2 cup milk
1 cup cottage cheese (creamed)	=	1/3 cup milk
2 Tbsp. cream cheese	=	1 Tbsp. milk

MILK SUBSTITUTES

Baking and run out of milk or cream? Remember that:

If the recipe calls for	You can substitute
1 cup coffee cream	3 Tbsp. butter plus 7/8 cup milk
1 cup heavy cream	1/3 cup butter plus 3/4 cup milk
1 cup whole milk	1 cup reconstituted non-fat dry milk plus 2-1/2 tsp. butter or margarine or 1/2 cup evaporated milk plus 1/2 cup water
1 cup buttermilk or sour milk	1 Tbsp. vinegar or lemon juice plus enough sweet milk to make 1 cup (let this stand 5 minutes before using)

TO USE HONEY INSTEAD OF SUGAR WHEN BAKING

1) Use 2/3 cup of honey for each cup of sugar called for.

2) For each cup of honey that you use, deduct about 3 Tbsp. of liquid from the recipe. (This does not apply to yeast bread.) In baked goods—add 1/2 tsp. soda for every cup subbed.

3) Reduce oven temperature by about 25 degrees and bake a little longer as honey tends to make baked goods brown faster.

To use honey instead of brown sugar, use some molasses with the honey.

FOOD AND RECIPE INDEX

A.C.T. 33
Aggression Cookies 28
Apple
　-baked 98
　-buying 117
　-"candied" 44
　-crisp, easy 60
　-juice 47, 100
　-soda 48
Apple Finger Jello 42
Apple Rings 43
Applesauce
　-in grocery 120
　-Lazybones 97
Applesauce Cake 67
Baby Food
　-commercial 128
　-in a microwave 93, 94
Bacon 95
Banana
　-bread 67
　-bread, milk free 107
　-buying 117
　-caramel 99
　-custard 56
　-frozen 33
　-smoothy 49

Berries 118
Blender mayonnaise 20
Bread
　-buying 125
　-Pita 126
　-zucchini 66
Breakfast Cereal
　-in grocery store 121
　-sugar content 122
Brown Sugar Frosting 70
Brownies 59
Caffeine 50
Calcium 105
"Candied" Apple 44
Cantaloupe 118
Carob 50, 70
Carrot Cake 65
Carrots 118
Center for Science in the
　Public Interest 29
Cheese/Bacon Sandwich 81
Cheese Cake Bars 61
Cheese Sandwich, melted 96
Cheese Chippies 99
Cheese Spread 36
Cheese Whiz 22
Cherry Balls 36
Chocolate 50

-cake 65
-drink in microwave 100
Chocolate Pops 35
Cold "C" Drink 51
Cookies
　-Aggression 28
　-Candy 28
　-Colossal 63
　-Clusters 64
　-Cottage cheese 62
　-Fortune 57
　-Great Gorpies 40
　-in the store 127
　-Melt-away 62
　-Peanut Butter 4
Corn-on-the-Cob 97
Cornell Triple Rich Formula 123
Cottage Cheese Cookies 62
Crackers 128
Cranberry Cupcakes 56
Cranberry Squares 59
Cream Cheese 132
　-sandwich 20
Cream Cheese Frosting 69
Creamsicles 34
Crunchies 40
Crunchola Mix 38
Crunchy Chocolaty Cookies 63
Cucumbers 119
Dairy 130
Danish Turnovers 58
Date Bars 62
Desserts 53-74
　-microwave 98
Dips 36
Drinks
　-en route 86
　-in school 24, 26
　-in stores 132
　-in a microwave 99
　-snack 46
Egg Sailboats 26
Eggs 131
　-Green Eggs and Ham 132
Fast Food Restaurants 88
Feingold Association 11
Finger Jello 42
Flour
　-enriching 123
　-white 123
　-whole wheat 124
Fondue, Peanut Butter 58
Fortune Cookies 57
French Toast 78
　-milk-free 107
Fried Chicken 81

Frostings 68
-chocolate/peanut butter 69
-colorings 71
-cream cheese 69
-Good 'n Easy 70
-milk-free 110
-peanut butter 69
Frozen Bananas 33
Frozen Foods 134
Fruit Leather 44
Fruit Nectars 47
Fruit Slurp 49
Fudge
-Super Fridge 59
Gorp
Granola Bars
-breakfast 39
-regular 39
-grape 40
Granola cereal 94
Grape Finger Jello 42
Grape Jelly 21
Grape Juice 47
Grapes 118
Great Gorpies 40
Hamburger Heroes 79
Hamburgers
-in a microwave 96
Honey "Cracker Jacks" 37
Hot Dogs 95, 134
Hot Instant "C" Mix 51
Ice Cream 71
-basic vanilla 72
-milk-free 111
-sundae 74
Ice Cream "Cookie" Cones 73
Jelly
-grape 21
Jell-Yo 57
Junket 54
Lact-Aid 106
Lettuce 119
Little-Bit-Of Chocolate-Bars 66
Macaroni Salad 82
Mayonnaise in a blender 20
Meat loaf 79
Melt-Away Cookies 62
Microwave Oven 93
-Fringe benefits 101
Milk 47, 87, 103
Milk Digestant 106
Milk Free Cake 110
Muenster Soup 95
Nitrite and nitrates 134
No-Bake Date Balls 41
Nutty Topping 70

Oatmeal 127
-in a microwave 95
-Raisin Cookies 63
Orange Froth 49
Orange Juice 46
Orange Juicesicles 34
Oranges 117
Pancakes, milk-free 107
Paradise Punch 48
Pasties 83
Peach Crumble 60
Peachy Delight 99
Peanut butter
-balls 17
-cookies 41
-milk-free cookies 111
-fondue 58
-in grocery 120
-frostings 68
-make your own 120
Peanut-Butter-Like-No-Other 22
Pears 118
Pineapple 118
Pineapple Upside-Down Cake 98
Pita Bread 126
Pizza 80
Polynesian Pops 34
Popcorn 37
-candy clusters 38
-honey "Cracker Jacks" 37
-Party Popcorn 27
Popsicles 33-35
Potatoes
-baked in a microwave 96
Poundcake 68
Pretzels
-soft 45
Pudding Mix 55
Quickie Cookies a la Stove Top 41
Raisin-Nut bars 61
Rennet 54
Saccharin 8
Salt 8
Sandwiches
-bread 17
-peanut butter 19
-tuna fish 19
-cream cheese 20
-spreads 22
School
-treats 25
-drinks 26
-birthday treats 27
-lunch program 29
Slippery Circles 43
Slush 49

Snow Cones 35
St. Patrick's Potatoes 119
Strawberry Ice 111
Sugar 4, 116
Sunshine Squares 43
Tomato Juice 48
Tomatoes 119
Triple Rich Formula 123
Tunabugers 108
Tuna Casserole 109
Tuna Fish
  -sandwiches 19
  -Swiss tuna on buns 96
  -in grocery 120
Tuna Baked Biscuits 80
Tuna Mousse 108
TV dinners 82
Unbirthday Cake 64
Un-Candy Bars 39
Unpizza Snack 99
Unrestricted Peanut Butter Cookies 111
Variety Pack Popsicles 34
Vegetables 97
  -green 119
Very Berry Ices 73
Water 46
Watermelon 118
Wheat Germ 125
Whipped Cream 68
Whipped Cream Graham Cake 64
Wholesome Pound Cake 68
Yogurt
  -frozen shake 49
  -frozen 56
  -about 130
  -uses 131
Yogurt Cheese 110
Yummie Balls 42
Zucchini Bread 66

NOTES

GREAT BOOKS FOR PARENTS

THE TAMING OF THE C.A.N.D.Y.* MONSTER
a cookbook by Vicki Lansky

*Continuously Advertised Nutritionally Deficient Yummies.

How to replace 'junk foods'. . . without tears.

Now Vicki Lansky has written her second book to make it easier for parents to feed pre-schoolers better foods. Vicki believes "less is better" when it comes to sugar, salt and additives, but you don't have to sacrifice convenience or good taste. More than 200 recipes and ideas are included for better snacks, desserts, baby sitter meals, and for eating enroute, brown bag lunches, microwave dishes, feeding milk sensitive children and shopping in supermarkets.

"A very useful cookbook emphasizing healthy alternatives to 'junk food'. A book for living... not sainthood."—Bev Kees, Minneapolis Tribune.
Spiralbound—$4.45 postpaid

FEED ME! I'M YOURS
by Vicki Lansky

America's #1 cookbook for new mothers.

This is the cookbook that is changing the way American babies and pre-schoolers are fed. It includes easy and economical ways to make baby food at home and delicious, nutritious alternatives to "junk food." And it's written in a delightful, down-to-earth style by Vicki Lansky and five experienced mothers. Over 200 child-tested recipes plus practical feeding advice. Spiral binding lays flat. Mothers love this practical, gifty edition.

"Chockful of ideas to make nutritious food irresistable to the playpen and fingerpaint set."—St. Paul Dispatch
Spiralbound—$4.00 postpaid

TO ORDER BY MAIL

end check or money order for total amount to:

MEADOWBROOK PRESS
6648 Meadowbrook Lane
Wayzata, Minnesota 55391

For combined book orders of six or more please write for quantity discount rates.

Book Price includes postage and handling	
THE TAMING OF THE C.A.N.D.Y. MONSTER by Vicki Lansky	@$4.45
FEED ME I'M YOURS by Vicki Lansky	@$4.00
RAISING HAPPY HEALTHY CHILDREN by Karen Olness, M.D.	@$4.45
DAVID WE'RE PREGNANT!! by Lynn Johnston	@$3.45
HI MOM! HI DAD! by Lynn Johnston	@$3.45
Baby Food Grinder	@$7.00

GREAT BOOKS FOR PARENTS